GREECE

an amazingly short history

by
ANDREW MEE

Travelbrief Publications

CONTENTS

INTRODUCTION
... AND AN APOLOGY

Geiá sas!
(Hello!)
In summer, flying into Athens, Salonika, or the islands, Greece looks horribly khaki. Except for the green spires of cypress trees and the white walls and red roofs of the houses, the landscape is empty, rough and parched, a jumble of ravines, rocks and tumbling screes.

Don't be put off.

It looks different from the ground, and more so in spring after cool rains have coaxed herbs and blossom from the crumbly soil. From ground level the brown is hedged in by mountains which step away into the distance, blue and purple and mysterious. A wild land - there are still bears and wolves in the Pindos Mountains. From the ground, Greece is very beautiful and it's easy to see why men have fought over it for at least three thousand years, and once out of the plane the evidence of ancient activity becomes apparent. Look carefully. Not all grey rocks are alike, some, on a second look, resolve themselves into walls, or perhaps into pieces of pediment or carved fragments torn from a nearby ruin.

Shouldn't such remains be in a museum somewhere? The Greeks are proud of their ancient heritage but they often treat it with infuriating carelessness. That's part of the charm of Greece, the paradoxical nature of the place. What we might put behind glass, they leave out in the burning sun. Perhaps this is because there's so much heritage and it goes back so far. Greece has the oldest culture in Europe and has the oldest writing too.

If, like me, you're a European, you probably think of Greece as the birthplace of much of your own culture and of many of your national institutions, in particular of democracy. In this sense, the history of Greece belongs to all of us.

Even the messy bits.

The ancient Greeks lived in a multitude of pushy, argumentative city states which squabbled endlessly. They were wonderful and infuriating yet by no means confined only to the area we now know as Greece. As Plato said, they lived 'like frogs round the pond', by which he meant round the whole of the Mediterranean. The history of Greece is not at all the same thing as the history of the Greeks but you can't understand one without understanding the other. This makes things both exciting and confusing. And to add to the confusion, even within Greece itself, it's a very diverse history. Even now, Salonika in the north and Athens in the south can seem like the capitals of different countries. If this book mentions, say, Istanbul, but doesn't mention a particular part of Greece which is your favourite, sorry, it's due to the nature of the beast.

Stories, myths and legends haunt the landscape of Greece, even in street names (if you can find them!). There are memories of muscular gods and beautiful goddesses, conquering kings and victorious queens, saints and soldiers, villains and heroes round every corner. Sadly, what applies to places applies equally to people. With four thousand years of history to cover, not all have made it into these pages. Please forgive me if your favourite philosopher, heroine, poet or bandit chief didn't make the cast list. I can only hope that the ones that appear will stand in for those left waiting in the wings.

Andrew Mee
April 2006.

MYTHS AND MAGIC

DIGGING UP THE PAST

In Brief - early Greece

BC

c.3,300	Bronze Age starts in Greece.
c.2100	Minoan culture starts on Crete.
c.1600	Mycenean civilisation starts.
1184	Fall of Troy.
1200	Dorian invasions from the north.
c.950	Start of the Iron Age in Greece.
c.800	City states start to form.
776	Tradional date of the first Olympic Games.
625	Democracy in some city states.
494	Persian wars start.
490	Battle of Marathon.
480	Battle of Thermopylae.
479	Greeks win the Persian wars.

Mrs Schliemann's Troy boy

The Time: a bright early morning in June 1873.

The Place: a privately-funded archaeological dig at an ancient mound called Hissarlik, in western Turkey, a short distance from the Aegean coast.

The Action: German millionaire Heinrich Schliemann trudges round the shadowy and unproductive trenches with his beautiful young wife Sophia.

It was the last day of the dig. Heinrich Schliemann was resigned to failure, having had no luck in his search over the previous three years. Suddenly, a sparkle in the shadows caught his eye. Not trusting the trench labourers, or himself to speak to them, he whispered to Sophia to dismiss the men for the day. He leapt down into the trench and began to dig, spellbound by the sight of gold still lustrous after three thousand years in the soil. His flashing knife dug out treasure after treasure, tumbling yellow metal in jittery haste into his wife's red shawl. Soon, in a wooden hut nearby, they were spilled out on the cloth: a gold mask and plate, gold filaments, buttons, hairpins, diadems, bracelets and brooches.

He draped the earrings and a pendant on his young wife. She looked as beautiful as Helen of Troy, whose gold he thought he'd found.

He'd been waiting for this day for forty-four years.

Heinrich's Homeric heroes

When he was the seven years old, Heinrich Schliemann, son of a poor German clergyman, had been given a wonderful picture book, a children's version of the *Iliad* and the *Odyssey*, two stories written originally by the ancient poet Homer. They told the story of a bitter war between the Ancient Greeks and their enemies, the Trojans, and of the Greek hero Odysseus's journey home to Greece afterwards. Most historians in the 1830s dismissed these books as myth, no more real than, say, Cinderella. Indeed, the poet Homer himself lived and wrote so long ago that even he could be a myth, a made-up name tacked on to tales collected from a hundred ancient firesides.

But the young Schliemann always believed that the *Iliad* told the story of real events. He told his chuckling father: 'When I am big, I shall go myself and find Troy and the king's treasure'. At nineteen he left home to make his fortune. By the age of forty-six he was rich enough to retire and to start looking for his fabulous Troy. Three years later he found the treasure.

Until almost the last days of his life, Schliemann believed that the gold really did form part of the treasure of Helen of Troy. He was wrong about that. We now know it was buried in the wrong level of the mound of Hissarlik and that it belonged to some other king or queen who'd died a thousand years before Helen of Troy was born. But that doesn't really detract from Schliemann's achievement. As a result of his efforts there can be no doubt that ancient Troy once existed. He opened the door to the history of the earliest Ancient Greeks.

The Greek Noah

The Greeks' own name for themselves, the 'Hellenes', has nothing to do with Helen of Troy. Hellen was the son of the mythical hero Deucalion and his wife Pyrrha. A bit like the Bible story of Noah, the god Zeus gave a warning that he meant to destroy mankind with a flood, so Deucalion built an ark to save himself and his wife. After the flood, they landed on Mount Parnassus (which became a holy

place) and began to repopulate the Earth. Hellen, their first son, was the ancestor of the Greek race, the 'Hellenes'.

'Greece' isn't a Greek word though - it's Roman. When Hellene settlers from the western province of Graia crossed the sea to southern Italy the Latin-speaking Romans called the newcomers 'Graeci', and people from the Hellenic region were said to be from 'Graecia', which became 'Greece'.

Minoan and Mycenean mysteries

Three years after his discovery of the 'Trojan' treasure, Schliemann began a dig at Mycenae on the Greek mainland. He went there because the *Iliad* said that a king of Mycenae had led the Greek fight against the Trojans. At Mycenae he uncovered evidence of a civilisation contemporary with Troy, a civilisation which had started way back in the remote past, around 1,600 BC. He even thought he'd found the golden mask of the Mycenean King Agamemnon, a central figure of the *Iliad*, although again he was mistaken.

Many details of Mycenean history are unknown, but they were certainly exceptional warriors and builders. The great stones of their walls were so massive that later Greeks thought they must have been built by a race of giants, the Cyclopes. Their civilisation seems to have been connected by trade and culture with a yet earlier and possibly Greek-speaking centre of power on the island of Crete. On Crete, a series of sumptuous palaces had been built and rebuilt before 1450 BC. The culture which built them is called 'Minoan', after the legendary King Minos, son of the god Zeus. According to myth, one palace had contained a labyrinth, or maze, which held the monstrous, bull-like Minotaur. The ruined ground plan of the largest palace, at Knossos, reminded another archaeologist,

Arthur Evans, of this ancient myth.

Nobody knows exactly why the palaces of Crete were rebuilt so often. But the Aegean is prone to earthquakes, and the huge eruption of the Thera volcano in about 1625 BC would have devastated the island. Also, and in the long run perhaps more importantly, the palaces were built without defences. They would have been easy prey to warlike seafarers.

The evidence of charred soil shows that, quite soon after victory over Troy, Mycenae was burned down. Other big cities fell too, including Iolkos, home of the legendary Jason and the Argonauts. By 1200 BC the Myceneans were fading from the historical scene. Again, no-one knows quite why, although about this time a race of invaders from the north took over. These new invaders are known as the Dorians. They settled mainland Greece, Crete and the shores of Asia Minor (modern Turkey) possibly pushing out earlier inhabitants. The next four hundred years was a Dark Age of chaotic refugee movements and defensive city-building

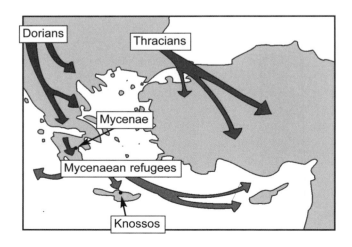

The City States

By 800 BC Greece was emerging from the Dark Age of the Dorian invasions. Greek traders and colonists plied the Mediterranean and the famous city states began to form. Small compared to modern states, each was usually a string of villages and farms set round some central fortification or 'acropolis', as at Athens. Sparta, on the Peloponnese, had an acropolis too, though the stand-up-and-fight Spartans didn't bother much with fortifications.

There were regular quarrels between states, but there was almost always a truce for the shared Greek passion for athletics. The traditional date for the first Olympic Games was 776 BC*. There were other athletics contests too: the Isthmian, Nemean and Pythian Games (these also had music, drama and poetry competitions). By 572 BC, all four festivals made up a four-year sporting period called the Olympiad. Contestants could win cash prizes, and celebrity athletes could make a good living.

It was a time of growing prosperity. The kings of Lydia in Asia Minor were the first to issue coins (about 650 BC) but the clever Greeks soon latched on. Money was much more

*There were other sporting competitions before this, but from 776 BC most of the Olympic results were recorded. The first ever winner of an Olympic race proper was Coreobus of Elis (a city in Olympia, appropriately enough).

convenient than bartering and it accelerated the spread of goods and ideas. By 600 BC, Greek coins could be found from India to Spain and this new wave of trading brought fantastic opportunities. Suddenly there were new, sophisticated building techniques, pottery, metalwork - even chickens, introduced from the Far East. And writing spread from the Levant (modern Lebanon). Writing was vital for the flowering of Greek culture. Without it, Homer would have been just another chanting, fireside storyteller.

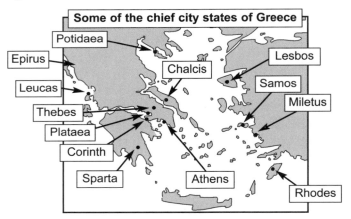

Some of the chief city states of Greece

The Persian peril

By 550 BC, the cities of Sparta and Athens were the most powerful Greek city states although all the other states were still separate 'countries', free to form alliances when the times demanded it - usually Sparta and others against Athens. Until 550 BC, the Greeks didn't need to club together to face common threats. There weren't any.

Not until the Persians arrived.

The incredibly sudden rise of Cyrus the Great's Persian Empire from 550 BC shocked the ancient world to the core. After just five years of fighting, the Persians ruled an empire stretching from India across to Ionia (the Aegean shore of modern Turkey) on the edge of the Greek world, where several Greek cities were gobbled up by the Persian colossus. Then part of Europe fell to the Persians for the first time. This was the state of Thrace to the north of Greece, captured by Darius I in 513 BC. The Persians were now very close to the Greek heartlands but, even at this late date, the disorganised Greeks hesitated to get involved. The idea of fighting on some other state's behalf was just too alien.

Finally in 499 BC, the Ionian Greeks revolted against Persian rule and asked for Greek help. The Spartans refused, saying they couldn't spare the men, but the Athenians felt they had to help out their Ionian 'cousins'. It might have been better if they had stayed at home. The Athenian gesture was half-hearted and acted as little more than an irritation to the Persians. In 494 BC, the Persians crushed the Ionian Revolt and destroyed Miletus, the great city of philosophers* and the foremost city of Ionia at that time.

Next, the Persian King Darius turned his vengeful eye on the Athenians.

*It's said that the philosopher Thales of Miletus (c.624-c.545 BC) was once asked the immortal question: 'If you're so clever, why aren't you rich?' Stung into action, he bought up all the olive presses in the region when his knowledge of weather patterns indicated a good harvest. With a monopoly on olive-pressing, he made a quick fortune, just to prove his point, then gave it away and returned to his simple life of philosophy.

Marathon men

The Persian war machine was terrifying. In 490 BC, Darius's galleys, loaded with warhorses and 30,000 men, landed on the Greek coast near Marathon. The Athenians were in a state of panic. They sent a runner called Pheidippides to Sparta to ask for help but the Spartans said they were too busy again, this time involved with a religious festival. Only the small force sent by Athens's neighbours, the Plataians, stood alongside the Athenians. Miraculously, the 10,000-strong Athenian and Plataian army was victorious. Under their brilliant general Miltiades, the Greeks made lightning strikes round and behind the Persian defences and routed the invaders. Hemmed in and driven back to the sea, the Persians lost 6,400 men compared to the Greeks' astonishing 192.

In the long run...

Pheidippides took only two days to run the 243 kilometres to Sparta. One legend says he was the soldier who, shortly after, ran from Marathon to Athens with news of the victory, this time weighed down by full armour. After gasping the words 'Rejoice! We win!', he collapsed and died. The modern marathon race is based on the twenty-six miles from Marathon to Athens.

If you're near Marathonas

Visit the site of the battle, marked by the Greek heroes' burial mound.

A league of heroes

Within ten years the Persians were back, this time with a much stronger force under Darius's son, Xerxes. Perhaps as many as 200,000 men and vast supplies of equipment were transported across the Bosphorus on a pontoon bridge of 674 boats lashed together.

Now even the Spartans were worried. They joined forces with Athens, and an alliance of Greek states called the Hellenic League was quickly put together. Sparta led most of the early fighting, especially at the Pass of Thermopylae (480 BC) where the southwards advance of the huge, Persian army was first challenged. There, in that barren rocky gulley, in an extraordinary display of courage, a mere 7,000 Greeks under the Spartan King Leonidas blocked the Persians' path until they could hold out no longer, and then, when all was nearly lost, the brave Leonidas fought on and died with his famous three hundred Spartans. They had held up the Persians long enough for the rest of the Greeks to escape.

> **If you're near Lamia, on the east coast**
> Visit the Thermopylae Memorial. The Battle of Thermopylae is marked with a burial mound, plus a bronze statue of King Leonidas.

Then it was Athens's turn. The wily Athenian leader, Themistocles, evacuated Athens, leaving it almost defenceless. He was banking on his newly-built navy, financed by the nearby Athenian silver mines at Laurium, to win the war. Athens was flattened but the gamble paid off. The Persian and Athenian fleets met at a narrow inlet near Salamis. Seated less and less comfortably on a golden throne on the nearby cliffs, Xerxes saw his 'invincible' navy smashed by the smaller Greek force. Uniquely, one of his ships was commanded by a woman, Artemisia of Halicarnassus. Though said to be a brave captain, she nevertheless fled the tightly-packed slaughter by ramming her galley straight through one of the other Persian ships.

If you're near Lavrio (ancient Laurium)
The two thousand odd mine shafts at Laurium were mainly worked by slaves in ancient times and some of the mines continued in production until they closed in the last century. A few are now open to visitors, housing the well-appointed Mineralogical Museum. Opposite the port of Lavrio is the fearsome prison island of Makronisos (see page 106).

The Persians had been driven off, but they were back for one more try in the summer of 479 BC. This time the Greeks were better prepared. A small but doughty Spartan contingent stormed through the Persian lines at the battle of Plataea, and at Mycale sea-going Greek soldiers once more smashed the Persian fleet. Xerxes slunk back to Persia, a beaten man.

The Persian threat was as good as over so the Greeks could get back to business as usual - fighting each other!

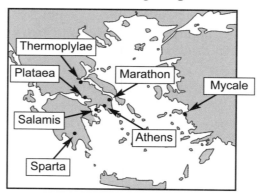

Greek Gifts

Classical Greece

In Brief - Classical Greece

BC

485-	Major playwrights active.
478	Delian League formed to counter the Persians.
461-29	Pericles's rule in Athens.
460-04	Peloponnesian Wars.
404-	Sparta dominant.
399	Death of Socrates.
371	Thebans beat Sparta to become dominant.
c.388	Plato founds his Academy in Athens.
338	Philip of Macedon defeats Athens and Thebes.

Democracy in action

Voting day in the fifth century BC. Excited crowds thronged to the Agora, the central meeting place in Athens. Aristides the Just, a hero of Marathon and Plataea and now a leader, made his way through the crowds. Voting was by *ostrakon*, a piece of broken pottery. A voter would scratch the name of someone he* wanted 'ostracised' or exiled on his piece of pot. On the way, a poor, illiterate man showed Aristides a blank *ostrakon* and begged him to scratch a name on it.

"Whose name should I write?" asked Aristides.

---

*Voters were always 'he' in Greece until women got the vote in 1952. During the Classical Age, all free-born (non-slave) adult Athenian men could vote. Ostracism was invented by Cleisthenes of Athens in about 508 BC to rid the city of politicians or generals who got too big for their boots. Unless voted back, an ostracised person had to live away from his home city for at least ten years. Even Cleisthenes may once have been ostracised

"Aristides," replied the poor man, clearly not recognising his helper.

"But why do you want Aristides ostracised?"

"I'm sick and tired of hearing him called 'the Just'!" complained the man.

Aristides, commendably devoted to the idea of democracy, silently scratched his own name and went on his way.

The Delian League

Aristides had been voted archon (ruler) of Athens after the Marathon victory in 490 BC but, in 482 BC, Themistocles, the leader who had commanded the Greek fleet at the Battle of Salamis, managed to get him ostracised. Strange behaviour for childhood friends who'd fought the Persians together - but that's the quarrelsome Greeks for you.

Recalled to Athens in 479 BC to help fight the Persians once more, Aristides was in command at the decisive Battle of Plataea. He then helped set up the Delian League, a Greek alliance against the common Persian enemy. It's said that Aristides' fair arrangement of subscriptions to the League was what earned him the nickname 'the Just'. Friends once more, Aristides and Themistocles worked together to strengthen Athens' defences, especially the 'Long Walls', battlements guarding the road from Athens to the port of Piraeus.

After 'Just' Aristides died in 468 BC, the Delian League became more and more 'unjust'. Membership stopped being optional and the treasury was moved to the Athenian Acropolis 'for safe keeping'. From the point of view of other members, donations began to seem more like taxes for the greedy Athenian Empire rather than contributions towards mutual defence. With its overwhelming navy ready to crush any resistance, Athens had begun to lord it over the other states.

Peloponnesian Wars

Sparta had never liked the Delian League, nor, come to that, democracy, which was just another fancy Athenian invention as far as they were concerned. Spartans thought the old ways were best and they stuck to tried and trusted rule by kings. They were a tough bunch, bred to be brave as lions but weak on conversation, reputed never to use two words where one would do*. Even today, a luxury-free lifestyle is said to be 'Spartan'.

Things came to a head in 460 BC, which was when the Peloponnesian Wars started, mainly between Athens and Sparta and their respective allies. These wars went on, with a few gaps, for the next fifty-six years. It was a gruelling conflict. Sparta and her allies had more men than Athens, but Athens had the bigger navy. In 431 BC, Sparta attacked Athens where it hurt most, cutting down her vital olive groves outside the Long Walls. Athenian peasants fled into their city which caused overcrowding, starvation and plague. Thousands died, probably of typhus.

The Golden Age

It seems astonishing that, despite a background of almost continuous war, Athens accomplished so much during these troubled years. The Golden Age of classical Greek culture lasted from 479 BC to 336 BC and Athens was at the centre throughout.

*Sparta was in the ancient Greek region of Laconia. It's said that when Philip of Macedon threatened to invade Sparta, he boasted: 'If I enter Laconia, I will raze it to the ground.' The Spartans' 'laconic' reply was: 'If...'

For much of this time (from 461 BC), Athens's leader was a radical democrat by the name of Pericles. He died during the siege of Athens in 429 BC. Among other things, Pericles invented paid jury duty so that even the poorest citizen could afford to be democratic. He also completed the Long Walls, begun by Aristides and Themistocles, and hired Hippodamus, probably the world's first town planner, to rebuild the port of Piraeus.

But the greatest of Pericles's achievements was the Parthenon, completed 432 BC. He brought in an outstanding designer, called Phidias, to lead a team of top sculptors, architects, painters and engineers and Phidias himself made the Parthenon's wondrous, forty-foot, gold and ivory statue of the goddess Athena*, Athens's own goddess. Several other beautiful buildings were completed at the same time as the Parthenon and Periclean Athens must have been a huge building site for much of the Golden Age. Pericles's building projects cost a fortune - but at least the contributions of the Delian League weren't paid in vain!

Pericles commissioned a statue of himself as well as a statue of Athena. He was shown wearing a helmet which was unusual. He suggested a helmet in order to hide an embarrassing deformity - his head came to a point on top.

If you're in Athens
The Monastiraki area to the north of the Parthenon is surprisingly untouristy. This was the heart of ancient Athens. There you will find the rather weird Tower of the Winds built around 50 BC.

You can see Pericles's statue in the Theatrical Museum.

---

*Athena, the special goddess of Athens, was also called Parthenos, 'the maiden'. 'Parthenon' means 'maiden's chamber'.

What a drama!
Theatre, from *theatron*, a place to look at things, was invented by the Greeks. It was partly an entertainment and partly a religious ritual and was very popular. Two thousands years before Broadway or the West End, they had revolving stages, hidden trolleys and cranes for special effects, and their ideas about drama still underlie much of what is written for TV and film. 'Tragedy' comes from *tragoidia*, 'goat-song', because in Greek plays the chorus (*khoros*) wore goatskins. 'Comedy' comes from *komoidia*, 'singing partygoers'. The writer Sophocles probably invented the 'casting' of particular actors for parts in plays.

When a young man and before he had risen to the top in politics, Pericles was the *choregos*, or producer, of tragedies by Aeschylus, one of the greatest Greek writers. Aeschylus more or less invented *drama*, which means 'play' in Greek, as well as realistic background scenery (*skene*). His death was appropriately tragic. An eagle, mistaking Aeschylus' shiny bald head for rock, dropped a tortoise it was carrying, expecting to break the tortoise's shell on the 'rock'. Aeschylus' head was smashed instead.

Pericles would also have known the other two famous playwrights of the age, Euripedes and Aristophanes. Grumpy Euripedes lived like a hermit in a cave near Salamis but Aristophanes was more of a party animal. He wrote wild satires and poked fun at his fellow playwrights. His play *The Frogs* is about a contest in the Underworld to see who was the best writer, Euripedes or Aeschylus, and so who deserved to be rescued from death. Aeschylus came out on top

Philosophers
Along with their love of drama, the Athenians took a close interest in philosophy which comes from the Greek for 'love of wisdom' and, at that time, meant enquiry into anything and everything. Pericles was a keen student. He was taught by Zeno of Elea, the first 'Stoic' philosopher, and by Anaxagoras, who described atoms and claimed that the Sun and stars were huge burning objects and that they had nothing to do with gods.

The famous philosopher Socrates was an Athenian and another friend of Pericles. Socrates was an atheist like Anaxagoras and that was a dangerous thing to be, even in Periclean Athens. Many Athenians thought that his atheism put the city in danger of heavenly reprisals, the gods being averse to non-believers. He was accused and convicted of corrupting the young and was ordered to kill himself by taking poison. He drank hemlock and died surrounded by his friends (399 BC).

Plato, one of Socrates' pupils, taught in Athens for nearly fifty years. He founded his garden 'Academy', where the word comes from, in about 388 BC. This was the most famous of all the Ancient Greek schools and it lasted for over nine hundred years. Plato's greatest pupil, Aristotle, invented zoology and was the first to formalise the idea of logic. He taught the young Alexander the Great in Macedon to the north and finally opened a rival school, the Lyceum in 335 BC*.

Gods almighty

The stories of the Greek gods may seem romantic, mysterious and perhaps quaint to us; to the Greeks, they were stories about real beings, the immediate causes of good luck or disaster. The gods were just like people with all their rages, passions and jealousies, but with absolute power. Keeping the gods on side was an everyday activity. Prayers, sacrifices, temple-building, you did whatever it took to keep them happy. There could be no opting out. Just one atheist in a city might bring the wrath of the gods down on everybody else.

If you're on Samos

An astonishing example of Greek engineering and mathematical skill can be seen at Eupalinos's Tunnel, a kilometre-long underground aqueduct built by slaves between 529-524 BC. It was used for piping water (in case of siege) from one side of the island to the other - straight through the central mountain. Amazingly, the diggers tunnelled from both sides at once to save time and met in the middle with almost no error. Due to the steep slopes, this is one sight not recommended for visitors who suffer from vertigo!

---

*One of Athens' later philosophers was Diogenes, the Cynic (from *kuon*, a dog). Poor and uncouth as a dog, he shunned worldly goods, lived in a large water-jar and didn't wash. When the Alexander the Great asked Diogenes what he could do for him, Diogenes is supposed to have answered: 'You can move out of the way of the sun and stop casting a shadow on me'

History

Pericles was fascinated by history as well as by philosophy, theatre, politics, art and architecture. Yet another of his friends was Herodotus, known as 'The Father of History', to whom we owe much of Greek history, as well as early maps of the world. Thucydides, soldier and admirer of Pericles, survived the Athens plague to become the main historian of the Peloponnese Wars. Another soldier-turned-historian, Xenophon, pupil of Socrates, picked up where Thucydides left off and was a crucial writer on Persia, Athens and Sparta.

Sparta strikes back

After Pericles' death in 429 BC, Athens's fortunes slowly went downhill. One leader, Alcibiades, defected to the Spartans after being accused of atheism. He persuaded the Spartans to join up with the Persians. However, the wildly adventurous Alcibiades was a fickle friend. He seduced the beautiful wife of the Spartan King Agis II and had to flee to the Persians. Eventually, he was pardoned by Athens and spent the next few years defeating the Spartan fleet in the Aegean. He returned to a hero's welcome in 407 BC.

But the end was in sight for Athens. Maverick leaders such as Alcibiades, however brilliant, were no substitute for hard Spartan grit. In 404 BC, a Spartan navy commander, Lysander, caught the Athenian navy beached at Aegospotami and used grappling hooks to capture 170 Athenian ships, which was most of the Athenian fleet. Alcibiades's nearby house was burned to the ground with him inside. The Athenians, trapped behind their fortifications, were forced to surrender and the triumphant Spartans pulled down the Long Walls, an act which the triumphant Lysander ordered performed to a musical accompaniment. He installed a pro-Spartan puppet government, called the 'Thirty Tyrants'.

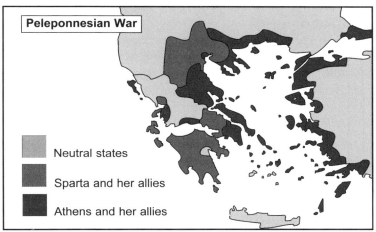

Peleponnesian War

Neutral states

Sparta and her allies

Athens and her allies

Athens's days as a great power were over. Her enemies rejoiced, but Athens's demise was in fact a misfortune for everybody. The Spartans never had enough money, soldiers or friends to be the leaders of the Greek world. They were argumentative, insular, old-fashioned and undemocratic. In 371 BC, Spartan control was ended by the Thebans at the Battle of Leuctra and for a while, Thebes took over as top Greek state while Athens and Sparta, together for once, fought to topple them.

And while the Greeks were busy fighting each other, a much bigger danger was growing in the north.

MACEDONIAN MAYHEM
PHILIP AND ALEXANDER

In Brief - Macedonian Greece	
BC	
359-36	Reign of Philip II of Macedon
336-23	Reign of Alexander the Great
323-240	Macedonian empire splits into separate kingdoms.
214-168	Macedonian/Roman wars.
146	Full Roman rule in Greece begins.

Philip's face found

In 1977, the celebrated Greek archaeologist, Manolis Andronikos, was excavating a burial mound in Macedonia, northern Greece. Like many ancient graves, it had been robbed in antiquity but, unusually, this mound contained an important-looking chamber which had been left untouched by tomb-robbers. Carefully burrowing into the chamber, unseen for thousands of years, Andronikos found a gold burial casket with the royal Macedonian Sun symbol on its lid. Nearby was some leg armour.

Inside the casket were partly burnt human bones. After facial reconstruction, the skull showed horrific injuries to its right side. Putting this together with evidence from the leg armour, which had been made for a man with one leg

---

If you're near Vergina

Vergina, burial place of the Macedonian monarchs, is 61 kilometres south-west of Salonika in Greek Macedonia. Some of the Royal Tombs are open to visitors and there are magnificent finds on display.

---

shorter than the other, there was no doubt in Andronikos's mind that he'd found the tomb of Philip II of Macedon. Philip was a warrior king who led from the front. Ancient texts mention that in one battle his sinews were cut making one leg shorter than the other, that he had a broken shoulder and a paralysed arm, and at the siege of Methoni in 354 BC, a catapult bolt shot from the city wall blinded his right eye.

Philip takes over

In ancient times, southern Greeks considered the kingdom of Macedon to be a barbarous backwater, hardly Greek at all*. The place was a political jungle. Macedonian kings always came from the same family but there was no right of succession. The king could choose his successor but others might not agree with the choice. This meant that Macedonian monarchs were forever on the lookout for assassins. Philip's older brother, King Alexander, had been murdered in 368 BC and in the confusion which followed, Philip had been sent to Thebes as a hostage.

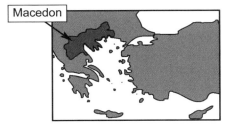

Macedon

*'Barbarous' comes from Greek, *barbaros*, to stammer or speak meaninglessly. Greeks thought non-Greeks could only grunt simple 'bar-bar' words. However, the royal house of Macedon, the Temenids, originally came from Argos in southern Greece.

Philip seized power in 359 BC. Having spent his teenage years as a hostage at Thebes, he had learned to respect Greek culture and he was determined to modernise Macedon along Greek lines. He revamped the Macedonian army, introducing Theban-style formations. This reformed army was a powerful weapon and with it he soon won control of all northern Greece. Then he built a new, Greek-style capital at Philippi, bringing in architects and sculptors from the south, and he married a Greek wife, Olympias, who bore him his famous son, Alexander, later known as 'Alexander the Great'. He even hired the Greek philosopher Aristotle as his son's tutor.

Over the next eighteen years Philip gradually spread his power southwards. Athens and Thebes formed an alliance against him but were defeated at the Battle of Khaironeia in 338 BC, after which Athens glumly expected the usual looting and massacres. But Philip had other plans. He sent his son, Alexander, to escort the honoured ashes of the fallen Athenians back to their home city and the following year, he set up his own, new Hellenic League, using charm as well as the threat of force to get his own way. Only the Spartans refused to join Philip's unified Hellenic Greece.

Philip needed the Greeks on his side because he had his eyes on an old enemy, the Persians. Unfortunately, he never saw the outcome of his plans. He was assassinated, possibly on the orders of Olympias, in 356 BC while celebrating the wedding of one of his daughters. Alexander and Olympias had been outraged when Philip took a new wife, even though polygamy was normal in Macedon and Philip had seven wives in total.

Alexander lost no time in putting on his father's crown and he soon proved that he was made of even sterner stuff, if that was possible. He crushed a Greek revolt then razed Thebes to the ground as a warning to the others.

If you're near Thebes

The unassuming modern town of Thebes has been built over the ancient acropolis from which the Thebans once ruled Greece during their period as most powerful city. Apart from Mycenean relics in the impressive archeological museum, Thebes's most arresting feature is the site of the fountain where the mythical Oedipus is said to have washed the blood from his hands after unknowingly killing his father while on his way to take up the Theban throne.

Alexander the Great

Queen Olympias was weird. She was a devotee of snake-handling cults and of mystic rituals involving Dionysus, god of ecstasy, possession and wine. She told Alexander that he wasn't Philip's son but actually was the son of a god who'd seduced her during a ritual. As a consequence Alexander carried an inflated sense of his own divinity for the rest of his life and became determined to live his own myth. He rampaged through life like an ancient hero. The Greek historian Plutarch said that:

> ...Alexander gave the impression of a madman, not giving orders sensibly, but as if in some kind of fit.

He was a driven man, driven to beat the achievements of his father, driven to beat the exploits of the ancient heroes, driven eventually to try to beat the gods themselves. He was always on the look-out for signs and wonders to show that he was favoured by the gods or, indeed, a god himself.

There's no doubt that he had an eye on the future. He wanted to be shrouded in myth. Possibly homosexual, he saw his dearest friend from childhood, Hephaestion, as a sort of reborn Patroclus, boyfriend of the legendary hero Achilles.

Alexander crossed to Persian-controlled Asia in 334 BC with a combined force of Greek and Macedonian troops. By this time, he was consciously following the footsteps of the ancient heroes of the *Iliad* before they attacked Troy. So much so in fact, that he slept with a copy of Homer's book under his pillow. Even back in the Fourth Century BC, there was a sort of tourist industry, and Alexander was one of the greatest tourists of all time. At Troy, where Greek mementos from a thousand years before were on display to visitors, he 'borrowed' the supposed shield of Achilles from the museum and carried it with him for the rest of his life. With his friend Hephaestion, he ran drunk and naked in celebration round Achilles' tomb.

Then the conquests began.

Alexander's army fought in Asia Minor, the Levant, in Egypt and in the Persian heartlands near modern Iraq. The Persian Emperor Darius III was pushed further and further back into his realm until he was finally cornered near the Caspian Sea and murdered by a local chieftain.

To the ends of the Earth
The Persian Empire became a part of the new, Macedonian Empire but Alexander couldn't stop. He went on, almost to China in the north-east and to India in the south. He took incredible risks. He was nearly killed during the siege of Multan, capital of the Punjab, when his chest was pierced by an arrow after a ladder collapsed, leaving him almost the only Greek in the citadel. The Greek historian

Arrian wrote:

> *...the wound bubbled with the escaping air. He was in terrible pain, but went on fighting. Suddenly there was a rush of blood from the wound, such as you get from a pierced lung, and Alexander, unconscious, slumped forward over his shield.*

But the gods were still with him. He was rescued in the nick of time when his generals broke through the citadel gates*. The defeated King Porus was set up as a puppet ruler and Alexander once again looked east. He wanted to go ever further, to the edge of the eastern world, to the 'Encircling Sea' of legend but, after ten years on the march, this was an adventure too far for his brave Greek heroes. Alexander had conquered most of the known world and surely that was enough? He reluctantly agreed to start the return journey*.

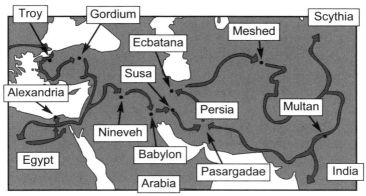

Now, finally, the gods began to desert him. The return from India was a disaster. Hephaestion died after an 'immoderate' drinking bout in 324 BC and Alexander went

---

*However, local Punjabi legend still has it that Alexander was in fact killed, and that his grave lies in India. His generals, it's said, were too frightened to reveal the truth and used a double to lead the army home.

mad with grief. He lay on his friend's body for a day and more, weeping and crying out to the gods. He never really recovered. He drank too much and made ludicrously overblown plans for a maritime route round Arabia, with a harbour big enough for a thousand ships. During a feast in the old Persian capital of Persepolis on 2 June, 323 BC, he reputedly consumed almost two gallons of wine. Fever set in and he died eleven days later, aged just thirty-two.

Hellenic kingdoms

The process of carving up the Hellenic Empire began immediately after Alexander's death when his generals divided it between them. Eventually, it developed into four separate kingdoms: Antigonid (Macedonian) Greece (including the Greek mainland), Seleucid Asia Minor and Persia, Ptolomaic Egypt and Pergamum. In all these kingdoms, Greek became the language of government, of trade, of the cities and of educated people.

Alexander's huge, ornate funeral carriage was hijacked by one of these generals while on its way to Macedon for a state burial. Ptolemy, the general in question, had claimed control of the southern part of the empire and he hoped that possession of the corpse would give his reign legitimacy. Alexander's body was taken to Egypt and there he was buried. The actual tomb is now lost but it may have been in Alexandria, site of the ancient world's greatest library, founded by Alexander in 332 BC.

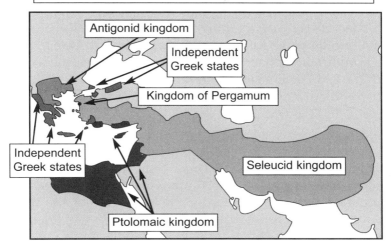

Hellenistic states with their subject territories in 240 BC

Antigonid kingdom

Independent Greek states

Kingdom of Pergamum

Independent Greek states

Seleucid kingdom

Ptolomaic kingdom

Rome!

Greece itself gave its Macedonian rulers a hard time over the next hundred years. One war followed another as the cities combined to fight for independence from their Macedonian masters or, alternatively, fought each other. But then a new and even more dangerous enemy loomed on the horizon. By 280 BC, Rome was a growing power.

To begin with, while Rome was still a small city state, the Roman Republic had its hands full in taking control of the rest of Italy. The first Greeks to be attacked were inhabitants of Greek colonies on the Italian mainland. The fighting was fierce. In 280 BC, Pyrrhus, King of Epirus in north-west Greece, went to their aid with an army of 25,000 men and some elephants. At first he defeated the Romans, though his victories came at such a cost in the lives of his own soldiers that the term 'Pyrrhic victory' has become a byword for disastrous success. But then Pyrrhus left Italy to fight other wars elsewhere and the Romans mopped up the Greek/Italian colonies.

Next, the Romans attacked Sicily where there was a major Greek colony at Syracuse. Syracuse fell in 212 BC after holding out against a ferocious siege with the help of its most famous citizen, Archimedes, a scientific and mathematical genius. During the last weeks of the siege, Archimedes supposedly held off the Romans almost single-handedly with a series of 'secret weapons', such as cranes to tip over approaching ships and polished shields used as 'heat-guns' to set ships on fire. When the city was finally overrun, the Roman general, Marcellus, ordered the valuable Archimedes to be taken alive. Sadly, Archimedes was stabbed to death by an ignorant Roman soldier after refusing to leave some geometry he was engrossed in. 'Don't disturb my circles!' were Archimedes' last words.

Now only the fading power of Macedon stood between the Romans and Greece itself.

'THE GREAT CITY'

THE EMPIRE OF BYZANTIUM

In Brief - Roman and Byzantine Greece

323-37	Constantine the Great sole ruler of Roman empire.
330	Founding of Constantinople.
392	Last of the Ancient Olympics.
395	Eastern and Western Roman Empires split by Diocletian.
499	Wild animal fights banned from the Hippodrome in Constantinople.
537	Haghia Sophia rebuilt by Justinian.
638-	Muslim warriors on the borders of the Byzantine Empire.
1204	Sack of Constantinople by Crusaders.
1453	Fall of Constantinople to the Turks.

Romans run riot

The Macedonian Wars with Rome lasted for forty-seven years but the outcome was never really in doubt. After the Battle of Pydna in 168 BC, Perseus, last king of Macedon, was taken to Rome and displayed in chains to the cheering crowds. The Romans went on to sack Corinth in 146 BC, marking the start of Roman rule in Greece proper.

The Romans loved Greece - that was why they conquered it. Once in charge, they carted off Greek treasures to furnish their villas back in Rome. They liked to think of themselves as a bit like the Greeks but not so soft. Sort of manly Greeks. The Roman Emperor Nero was so keen on Greek culture that he entered for the lyre competition, the poetry contest and the chariot race at the Olympic Games of 67 AD. He won of course. Who was about to argue with a lunatic who murdered his mother, kicked his pregnant wife to death and apparently burnt down Rome for the fun of it? Thankfully, not all Roman Emperors were as outrageous as Nero. Hadrian (of 'Hadrian's Wall' fame) rebuilt many ancient Greek ruins, notably the biggest one, the Temple of Zeus in Athens, first started 650 years before.

If you're in Athens,
Hadrian's Arch leads to the huge Temple of Zeus. Although only 15 of the original 104 Temple columns remain, the scale of the building is staggering.

The two Roman Empires

By 300 AD, the Roman Empire had become an unwieldy giant, bloated by a hundred successful wars of conquest. It was split into two halves by the Emperor Diocletian (306 AD) to make administration easier: a western half and an eastern, mainly Hellenic half. After the split, there was a power struggle with, at one point, as many as six emperors claiming the throne, but eventually, a brilliant general called Constantine the Great came out on top (323 AD). Constantine ruled both halves of the Empire. There were two very crucial differences in how he managed things compared to previous rulers:

1. Christianity became the official religion of the Roman Empire.
2. He built a new capital in the Greek half, at the Greek port of Byzantium on the European shore of the Bosphorus.

Originally a tiny sect and much persecuted by the Romans, by 323 AD Christianity had grown into an important new religion with vast numbers of followers, Constantine himself probably becoming a convert around 312 AD. When, in 330 AD, he inaugurated his new capital city, called 'Constantinople' (modern Istanbul) after its founder, he made sure it would be a Christian city. It had at its centre the Milion, the First Milestone, from which all distances in the Empire were to be measured. On top of the Milion, was placed the True Cross of Christ, taken from Jerusalem, to show that Christianity now stood at the very centre of the Empire.

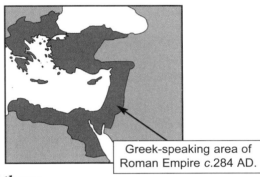

Greek-speaking area of Roman Empire c.284 AD.

Fading Athens

Greek was the main language of the eastern half of Constantine's Empire but, paradoxically, Athens and mainland Greece stagnated. The wealthy, dynamic parts of the Greek world lay elsewhere, in Constantinople itself and in great cities such as Alexandria and Ephesus.

The stagnation had started years earlier. By Constantine's time, Athens had been living off its past for centuries. It survived as a destination for cultural tourists who were interested in its ancient glory and as the home of various schools of philosophy. Rich Romans visited as part of their education and emperors such as Hadrian donated money, but no one who mattered ever stayed for any length of time. Worse was to follow.

Unfortunately for Greece, most of its great monuments and treasures were pagan. Its temples and statues were now the symbols of a corrupt and out-of-date religion. The temples were neglected. Paint flaked from the Parthenon and it began to take on the bleached, white appearance which it has today along with countless other classical ruins. Finally, in 393 AD, the Christian Emperor Theodosius closed down the Olympic Games, the greatest of the pagan festivals. From now on, Greece was a backwater and had no particular reason to think itself important.

For better or worse, the rich, cruel, highly-cultivated pagan culture of ancient times was fading away and Greece with it. In 491, the Emperor Anastasius I, a pious Christian, came to the throne. He hated all impious forms of entertainment and in 499 he banned wild animal fights in the Hippodrome at Constantinople, where chariot races were held. There were riots but the ban held. Finally, in 529, the Academy at Athens and other pagan schools were closed on orders from the Emperor Justinian.

Standing alone
By now, the western half of the Roman Empire was fading away, destroyed by large, fair-haired warriors from the

north of Europe. But the eastern half kept going, and the longer it lasted, the more Greek and the more Christian it became. Later historians called it the 'Byzantine' Empire, after the ancient Greek colony on which the city of Constantinople was founded. All other ancient empires having been destroyed, it alone remained, the largest and most advanced power in the world, except possibly China. The language of government was Latin until quite a late date but the language of the merchants and of the cities was Greek, even though Greece itself was fading.

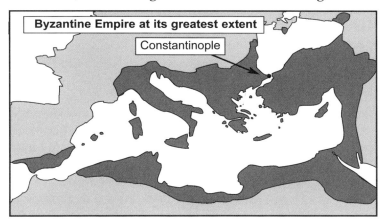

Byzantine Empire at its greatest extent

Constantinople

Pantomime Hooligans
Greatest of all the Byzantine Emperors was Justinian who closed down the schools in Athens. He came to the throne in 527. By that date, the there were churches everywhere. He built a massive and magnificent church called Haghia Sophia ('Holy Wisdom') in the centre of Constantinople, right next door to the royal palace.

But pagan culture didn't roll over and die overnight. In particular, chariot racing in the Hippodrome next door to the church of Haghia Sophia stayed popular. Chariot racing was followed with an intensity which is hard to imagine today even when judged by the behaviour of some modern football fans. There were two teams, the Greens and the Blues, and almost everyone, even members of the royal family, followed one side or the other. Even far flung cities such as Ephesus, and quite possibly Athens, had their Green and Blue supporters. Greens and Blues took sides over almost everything, even who were the best actors. In May 501, at the pantomime dancing festival of Brytae, riots between them had led to over 3,000 deaths.

In his early life, Justinian had been a Blue, for political reasons because Blues were then more powerful. His wife, the Empress Theodora, was the daughter of a Green bear-keeper, and a former exotic dancer and actress. One might have expected, given that they had first-hand knowledge of both factions, they might have been able to handle the Greens and Blues quite easily, but not so. In 532, when two thugs from the rival teams survived being hung for murder, Blue and Green fans demanded free pardons for them and smashed down the doors of the prison. Chanting their charioteering slogan, 'Nika!' ('Win!'), they rampaged through central Constantinople, burned down the great church of Haghia Sophia and, back in the Hippodrome, proclaimed an elderly royal relative, Hypatius, as Emperor. Justinian appealed for calm from the imperial box but was shouted down. Together with his top advisers, he was about to flee the city.

At this point, Theodora took a hand. She told Justinian to stand up to the thugs or be shamed forever. The Emperor's great general, Belisarius was thrown into the fray and, fortunately, the fragile peace between the fans broke down and Blues and Greens began to fight each other on the race track. By the end of the day, 30,000 rioters lay dead and the *Nika* Revolt was over.

Justinian built a new church of Haghia Sophia, on the site of the previous one but even bigger. It was the largest building in the world for the next thousand years. Meanwhile General Belisarius pushed the western borders of the Empire out as far as the Strait of Gibraltar, regaining Sicily, southern Italy and finally Rome itself, so that the original capital of the Roman Empire became a subject of the eastern, Greek half.

If you're in Istanbul
Justinian's rebuilt Haghia Sophia lies at the heart of the Sultanahmet district of central Istanbul, opposite the Blue Mosque. It was designed by the Greek mathematician Anthemius of Tralles and the engineer Isidore of Miletus and it incorporated precious marbles from all over the Byzantine Empire.

Minarets added by the Turks

Orthodoxy
The Greek Orthodox (means 'right believing') Church, or Eastern Orthodox Church as it is also known, is the main Church of Greece, Bulgaria, Serbia and Russia and other countries in south-east Europe. Its music is extraordinarily

beautiful, its churches are elaborately painted and its bearded priests in their tall hats are free to marry, although not its monks perched in their remote monasteries on cliffs and jagged hillsides throughout the Greek peninsula.

If you're in central Greece
The Meteora region in north-west Thessaly contains some of the most spectacular monasteries in Greece. The Meteora monasteries were founded in the Middle Ages after some Orthodox monks retreated from the more famous but less secure Athos peninsula which had become dangerous due to the raids of Turkish pirates. The Meteora monasteries perch on towering, inaccessible pinnacles of rock. 'Meteora' means 'suspended in air'.

For centuries after the birth of Christ, the Greek Church and the Roman Catholic Church were one and the same, but the unity was always strained. Greeks and other easterners never gave the Pope in Rome the respect he thought he deserved. In the west, the Bishop of Rome (one of the Pope's titles) was thought of as a unique stand-in for God's authority on Earth; to easterners he was only first among equals - just a rather special bishop in fact. In the Greek world, people looked towards their own leader, the Patriarch, who led services in the great church of Haghia Sophia in Constantinople. The music and the styles of service still sung in churches from Athens to Moscow are derived from the great religious rituals of the Byzantine Empire.

Troubles and tensions between smooth-shaven popes and the bearded patriarchs developed gradually over the years. Most of the disagreements centred around weird points of religious doctrine most of which seem positively insane to modern ears. Things came to a crisis in 1054 when a delegation from Rome arrived in Constantinople and the two sides became locked in a vicious argument. Insults were hurled back and forth and eventually the Roman delegation retreated to Rome to lick their wounds. This date is taken as the start of the 'Great Schism' between east and west which still divides the Christian world, predating Rome's other split, with the Protestants, by over five hundred years. The 'Great Schism' meant that western Roman Catholics felt free to regard Greek Orthodox Christians as heretics and sinners.

The Fourth Crusade

Meanwhile, Justinian's golden age hadn't lasted. After he died the Byzantine Empire suffered repeated invasions and a slow loss of land. In the east, Mohammed was born (c.570) and, by 700, most of what is now the Arab world had been taken over by the Muslims, including the Holy Land of Palestine. In the west, by 1200, much of the Greek peninsula and its islands had been split into a motley bunch of little states run by Catholic Franks, Venetians and Genoans who extracted every ounce of tax they could from their Greek Orthodox subjects.

The Crusades were an attempt by the Catholic west to win control of Palestine from the Muslims. During the first three Crusades (1095-99, 1147-48 and 1189-92), the crusading armies marched down through the Balkans, through Byzantine territories and on into the Holy Land without causing too much trouble for the Greeks. But, in 1204, the Venetian sponsors of the Fourth Crusade decided to capture Constantinople while they were passing. On Easter Day 1204, drunken, bloodstained 'Frankish' soldiers draped a prostitute on the Patriarch's throne in Haghia Sophia and danced around her for a laugh. Filthy horses and carts trundled in and out of the churches, carrying away priceless relics and vestments which still adorn cathedrals in France, Germany and Italy. The Greeks never forgave the Venetians for the horrors of the Fourth Crusade and, although Greek emperors regained the throne sixty years later, the Byzantine Empire never properly recovered.

Greece had lost its protector.

The coming of the Ottomans

Shortly after the Greeks regained control of Constantinople from the Crusader kings, they had to face a renewed threat from the east, from tough Muslim tribesmen. These Turkish tribesmen fought on horseback and had been a danger for years, but around 1320 they gathered around a new and dynamic leader, or *bey*, by the name of Osman or 'Othman'. In 1352, the 'Ottoman' Turks, named after Othman, crossed the Dardanelles and took Gallipoli. Fifty years later, they were in control of most of the peninsula of Greece and the once-grand Byzantine Empire had been reduced to a small patch of land around Constantinople and a few far-flung outposts.

Sultan Mehmet II, called the Conqueror, came to power in 1451, aged nineteen. The Byzantine Emperor at that time was middle-aged Constantine XI. Constantinople itself was on its last legs, economically strangled by the encircling Turks. As Mehmet himself put it:

> It is no longer a city, but a name, an enclosure of plants and vineyards, worthless houses and empty walls, most of them in ruins.

But it was still a name worth capturing and the young Sultan was determined to make *his* name. The fight was a bit one sided though. A roll call before the battle listed just 4,983 Greeks against the Sultan's besieging army of over 300,000. And the Turks brought weapons that the mighty walls of Constantinople had never seen before - cannon. Specially built for the job, these monsters threw stone balls, some weighing half a ton. The largest of the great guns was so enormous and difficult to handle that it could only be fired seven times a day.

Incredibly, the City held out. A few Christian ships even managed to run the Turkish blockade and bring in supplies. In desperation, the Sultan dragged seventy galleys overland to the Golden Horn, a sea inlet closer to the defences, but still the defenders hung on. After six weeks, with rumours of a Venetian relief fleet on the way and discontent brewing in the ranks, Mehmet gambled everything on an all-out attack. He sent in massed ranks of irregulars. Wave after wave of Slavs, Hungarians, Kurds and the like, even a few Greeks, threw themselves at the walls, urged on by the whip-wielding Turks behind. Some surged in when a cannonball breached the wall, others burst through a gate tragically left unguarded after a brief Greek sally. The Sultan's crack troops, the janissaries, stormed in and the end of the siege was certain. There was mayhem and murder on May 29 1453.

There are conflicting accounts of the death of Constantine XI, last of the 'Roman' Emperors. In the frenzied mêlée of a medieval battle, nobody stopped to take notes. It's likely that when the Turks poured into the city through the breached walls, he stripped off his Imperial armour and fought as a common soldier, dying with his subjects in the burning ruins.

It was a dreadful day, a Tuesday. In Greece, Tuesdays are still considered unlucky.

TURKOCRACY
LIFE UNDER THE OTTOMANS

In Brief - Ottoman rule

1520-66	Reign of Sultan Suleiman the Magnificent.
1523	Turks capture Rhodes.
1529	Turks control the Greek Pelopponese and the Aegean.
1570	Turks capture Cyprus.
1571	Battle of Lepanto.

The 'Tax of Children'

For the next 350 years, the Greeks were a conquered people, their Mediterranean heartland a frontier in the wars between the Venetians and the Ottomans. There was little to choose between these two enemies. Indeed, despite the Greeks and the Venetians both being Christian, many Greeks actually preferred Muslim rule. The Venetians imposed much stiffer taxes than the Turks. Also, the sacking of Constantinople in 1204 remained a bitter memory.

If you're on the island of Crete

The beautiful port of Chania, Crete, was Venetian from 1205 to 1669, when it fell to the Turks after reputedly the longest siege in history - twenty-four years. It has the best preserved Venetian town and harbour outside Italy.

But one Muslim tax was bitterly resented by most Greeks, the *devshirme*, the 'tax of children'. Ottoman officials would tour the Empire choosing Christian boys to be taken away to be slaves. The boys were converted to Islam and set to work for the Sultan. The strongest were trained as soldiers, the dreaded janissaries, spreading fear far and wide; the smartest became civil servants. In either case, the parents would probably never see their boy again.

High fliers

Paradoxically, since Greece had become the province of a foreign empire, the *devshirme* was one way for boys of Greek origin to succeed on a wider stage. At that time in Turkey, slavery could be much less humiliating than it sounds and slaves were often freed. A clever Greek boy could rise to a top job, perhaps as a *dragoman* (interpreter) or even as a *vizier* (counsellor). Some were trained in art or building. The Greek-origin architect Sinan, greatest of the Ottoman architects, built eighty-one mosques, including the Suleimaniye, finished in 1557, the most important mosque in Constantinople.

Even more exalted than Sinan, although not exactly a product of the *devshirme* system, was Ibrahim Pasha, one of the most distinguished Greek slaves in the history of the Ottoman Empire. In 1499 when six years old, he was kidnapped by pirates and sold to a rich Turkish widow in Lydia. Given the name Ibrahim and converted to Islam, he became a page at the imperial court and grew to be a bosom pal of Sultan Suleiman the Magnificent. He rose to become Grand Vizier and became almost as powerful as the Sultan himself. Eventually, Suleiman took offence when Ibrahim started to call himself 'Sultan'. Ibrahim was assassinated in the 'traditional manner' - strangled with a bowstring cord by a gang of deaf mutes.

It wasn't only Greek boys who contributed to Ottoman culture. Although the *devshirme* was restricted to boys, there were plenty of Greek slave girls as well. As a young girl, Kosem was abducted from Corfu, forced to join Sultan Ahmed's harem and was the mother of two Sultans: Murad the Victorious and Ibrahim the Mad. Through her sons she dominated the empire for nearly forty years, until, in her eighties, she too was put to death with the cord. Toothless, she gummed her murderers' hands to shreds before she suffocated.

Kosem was part of an interesting tendency. Since Ottoman sultans usually had their children by slave girls and those girls were often Greek, there must have been almost as much Greek blood as Turkish in the veins of the Sultan himself.

Red beard

The janissary slave regiments of the Ottomans were almost unbeatable, especially during the reign of Sultan Suleiman the Magnificent. In 1523, he took Rhodes from the Crusader Knights of St John and, by 1529, he was in charge of the Greek Peloponnese and the Aegean. Only the Venetians held onto a few small footholds on the Greek mainland and on the islands, but they never had enough men to beat the vast Ottoman Empire on the battlefield. They relied instead on their brilliant navy to hold their fortress trading posts.

> ### If you're in Rhodes
> The magnificent walled city of Rhodes Old Town is dominated by the Palace of the Grand Masters (leaders of the Crusader Knights of St. John 1309-1522). It was restored to its former glory by Mussolini and is now a museum filled with extravagant mosaics and sculptures.

To counter the sea-going Venetians, Suleiman built new shipyards in Constantinople and, the Turks being poor sailors, he hired Barbary corsairs, fierce Muslim pirates from the North African coast, to command his navy (1534). The cruelty and cunning of these corsairs was legendary. Most feared of all was Barbarossa, Suleiman's admiral, himself the son of a janissary soldier by the widow of Greek priest. Already sixty-seven when he joined up with Suleiman, over the next twelve years Barbarossa devastated the coasts of France and Spain with his sleek black ships*.

Selim the Sot

Suleiman was followed on the throne by his heavy-drinking son, Selim the Sot who, in 1570, turned his bleary gaze on Venetian-ruled Cyprus. Cyprus was the source of his favourite tipple and Selim's closest friend and adviser, a Portuguese Jew called Joseph Nasi, suggested capturing the Cypriot vineyards so he wouldn't have to pay Venetian taxes on Cypriot wine. 50,000 Turkish lives were lost taking the Venetian fortress at Famagusta and afterwards, Selim's men took horrible vengeance on the Venetians. The Venetian commander, General Marcantonio Bragadino, was flayed alive, his skin was filled with straw and the grotesque stuffed object was hung from a yardarm.

At the time it must have seemed that Ottoman power was

*'Barbarossa' means 'Redbeard' in Old Sabar, the pirate language of the Mediterranean. Strangely, Barbarossa didn't actually have a red beard at all. It was his older brother's nickname. Barbarossa took it over when his brother, also a pirate, was killed.

invincible and the Greeks would be under the Ottoman thumb for ever. But Selim's conquest of Cyprus proved to be one conquest too many for the Christian west. A joint Italian, Maltese and Spanish fleet, organised by the Pope and led by Don Juan of Austria, bastard half-brother of the Spanish king, was sent to Lepanto, in the Gulf of Corinth, with orders to crush the Turkish fleet once and for all.

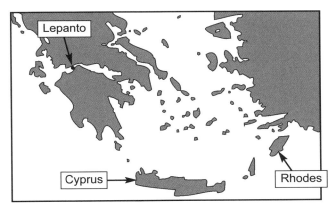

Lepanto

Battle was joined on 7 September 1571. That morning, under clear, blue skies, 485 oar-powered galleys moved slowly towards each other across the calm waters of the Gulf. The two opposing flagships, *Real* and *Sultana*, crashed head on, followed by the rest of their fleets, and soon the sea was a tangled chaos of ships. Many of the oarsmen on both sides would have been Greek - galley slaves on the Ottoman side and criminals, mercenaries and a few volunteers on the Christian side.

It was the last great sea battle using galleys and the fight went on for four hours, each hour seeing the bloody deaths of 10,000 men. The sea turned red with blood and there were countless individual acts of heroism. When artillery officer Federico Venusta's hand was blown apart by a grenade, he chopped off the trailing ends, had a chicken carcase strapped to the stump and went back to the fight, declaring:

Let the right hand avenge the left!

When it was over, the Turks had been soundly defeated. The Battle of Lepanto put an end to wholesale Muslim expansion in the Mediterranean and marked the turning of the tide for the Ottoman Empire - and for the Greeks.

If you're at Nafpaktos (old Lepanto)
Situated on the beautiful Gulf of Corinth and facing the blue Peloponnese mountains, modern Nafpaktos is the nearest town to the site of the Battle of Lepanto, Lepanto being its old Venetian name. The picturesque, fortified harbour is overlooked by a fine Venetian fortress.

From the lighthouse
The Ottomans never sorted out a successful way of selecting and educating new sultans. By 1700, their Empire was in serious decline, each sultan seemingly madder or more stupid than the one before. Greece, a province within this failing empire, found itself appallingly badly governed. Local clan chiefs were often too tough for the Sultan's officials to control. Local leaders, called *Pashas*, or *Beys* in Turkish, were given the job of collecting the Sultan's taxes skimming off their own share as they went along.

During this period, while Greece sank back into medieval squalor, the richest and most successful Greeks lived in Constantinople, in the lighthouse district along the Bosphorus, a sort of Millionaire's Row of the Ottoman Empire. By 1700, 'Phanariot' Greeks (from the Greek *phanarion*, a lighthouse) had taken over the role of Grand Dragoman ('interpreter') and made it more or less hereditary. Most diplomacy went through the Dragomans, who also directed the Ottoman admirals at sea. By 1800, Phanariot Greeks were actually running many of the Greek islands as well as Romania and parts of mainland Greece.

It was only a matter of time before some of these rich, educated Greeks began to wonder if, perhaps, it was time to throw off the Turkish shackles, however comfortable they might be for a few.

REVOLUTIONARY RUMBLINGS

SPARKS WHICH LIT A FIRE

In Brief - Start of the Greek Revolution

1770s   Revolutionary writers start to be active in
         Vienna and other cities.
1787   Ali Arslan, 'Lion of Ioannino', becomes Pasha.
1814   The 'Friendly Society' formed.
1821   Alexander Ipsilantis raises the flag of revolt
         in the north.

Dreamers

In 1797, Vienna, capital of the creaking Austro-Hungarian Empire, was a repressed city, a city of intrigues where nationalists from a multitude of ethnic groups wove their dreams of freedom in smoky coffee houses or in the foyers of elegant concert halls. One such was Rigas Velestinlis, a well-mannered forty-year-old from Thessaly. In the daylight hours, tall, dapper Velestinlis was the respectable secretary of an Austrian baron but at night he met fellow idealists in gloomy cellars and dark cafes, briefed underground printers and produced subversive songs, books and pamphlets. Velestinlis believed that the time was ripe for Greek independence. In his plans there was even room for the Turks. He wanted them to rebel against their corrupt Sultan.

Sadly, Velestinlis never saw his dreams made flesh. In December, an informer handed his secret papers to the authorities, and they in turn passed him over to the Turks.

The end for Velestinlis came six months later. He was brutally murdered and his body was thrown into a river. But his writings lived on, not least his rallying call to the Greek people:

Better one hour of free life than forty years of slavery and prison!

By 1797, the Ottoman Empire was sinking fast, on its way to becoming the 'sick man of Europe'. At last, Greeks such as Velestinlis were able to imagine an end to their subjugation. But unfortunately, not all such dreamers were as fair minded as him. The other great prophet of Greek independence was an utter contrast. Adamantios Korais, born to a wealthy family in Smryna (modern Izmir), was a rabid hater of Turks, perhaps because of the harsh beatings handed out by his Muslim teachers. Dry, gaunt and sunken-eyed, he was an obsessive hypochondriac, forever fussing over his bleeding gums. He spent much of his life in France, writing modern Greek versions of ancient Greek writings, common knowledge of which had pretty much died out under Turkish rule. Korais was adamant that the Greeks had to know their own history if they wanted to throw off the Turkish yoke.

The Friendly Society

In Greece, secret societies began to spring up. Members argued over how to bring about Greek independence and about the benefits which would come from an end to Turkish rule. The most important of these societies was the *Philiki Etairia*, or 'Friendly Society', began in 1814, but its harmless sounding name was just a cover. Its real aim was to build up membership until it became an unstoppable force, then to explode into rebellion everywhere at once. By 1818, it had enlisted some big names to lead the rebellion, such as a southern clan leader called Petrobey Mavromihalis, and a tough ex-mercenary, called Theodoros Kolokotronnis, but more were needed.

In the north, the Society settled on the Phanariot General, Alexander Ipsilantis, a senior figure in the Russian army. Brave as a bull, young and hot-headed, Ipsilantis had lost his right arm fighting for the Tsar. He was keen to get started and was ready to attack from his Russian base. But when would be the right time?

Enter the appalling Lion of Ioannina ...

Revolt!

Ali Arslan was an Albanian Muslim, born into a family of brigands in 1750. He was crafty, greedy and cruel. He'd been a feared sheep rustler by the age of fourteen and, such was his ruthlessness, by twenty he and his gang of cut-throat robbers and extortionists were in charge of all Albania. Nobody was safe from this short, fat, piercingly blue-eyed fiend. When a bishop's niece, Euphrosyne, was accused of seducing his young son Mukhtar, he had her tied up in a sack and drowned, some say because she spurned his own advances. Ali's exploits eventually came to the notice of the Ottoman Sultan Abdulhamid in distant Constantinople. Abdulhamid thought Arslan would be a cheap way to control a difficult part of his empire and made him Pasha of Ioannina (1787). Unfortunately for the Ottomans, the 'Lion of Ioannina' was nobody's to control. By 1819, he was running much of western Greece as a gangster fiefdom and posed a direct threat to Ottoman rule. A new sultan, Mahmud II, sent in troops to crush the upstart.

Here was the opportunity that the Tsar's general,

Alexandros Ipsilantis, had been waiting for. While the Sultan was preoccupied with Ali Pasha, the one-armed general seized his chance. He raised the flag of revolt and crossed into the Ottoman territory of Moldavia in early March 1821. By April he'd gathered an army of two thousand men and was moving on Turkish-held Bucharest. He confidently expected the local, Slav population of what is now Romania to join him since they too were oppressed by the Ottomans.

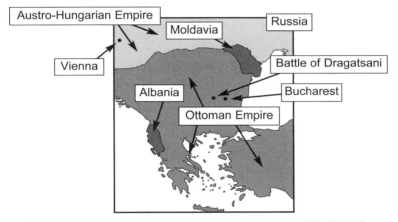

Austro-Hungarian Empire

Moldavia

Russia

Vienna

Battle of Dragatsani

Albania

Bucharest

Ottoman Empire

If you're in Ioannina:

Ioannina, a large town in the west, has some of Greece's best preserved Ottoman remains, including the Aslan Pasha mosque. The monastery of Ayios Pantelimon where Ali Pasha died is on the nearby island of Nisi.

But the local Slavs let Ipsilantis down. As far as they were concerned there was very little to choose between a rich Phanariot Greek and an Ottoman. Why fight for the Greek Ipsilantis just to swap one lot of tyrants for another? Without support from the locals or the Russians, Ipsilantis's small army was smashed by the Turks at the Battle of Dragatsani (June 1821). But this was not the end for the Greeks. Alexandros Ipsilantis might have failed but the spark of revolt had been lit. His campaign proved an excellent diversion for events in the south.

In January 1821, local revolutionary leaders called a meeting in the Peloponnese town of Vostitsa. By March, things were becoming interesting.

THE WAR OF INDEPENDENCE
FREEDOM FIGHTERS AND THEIR FRIENDS

In Brief - the War of Independence	
1821	Bishop Germanos raises the rebel flag.
1821	Philhellenes flock to join the war.
1822	Ali Pasha killed.
1822	Massacre of Chios.
1824	Lord Byron dies at Mesolongi.
1825	Ibrahim Pasha lands in Greece.
1827	Battle of Navarino.
1828	Ioannis Kapodistrias arrives in independent Greece.

The flag is raised

Tradition says that the Greek War of Independence started on March 25 1821, when the tall, black-bearded Bishop Georgios Germanos raised a rebel flag in the tiny village of Kalavrita on the Peloponnese.

If you're in the Peloponnese
The museum at the monastery of Agias Lavras, six kilometres southwest of Kalavitra, houses the traditional rebel flag.

Most other churchmen were against the uprising. Back in Constantinople, the Orthodox Patriarch, Grigorios V, even excommunicated the ringleaders. Not that it did him any good. When news of the revolt was brought to Sultan Mahmud II, he executed Grigorios and had his body dragged through the streets of Constantinople, a stupid and brutal act which only served to inflame Greek passions further. Religious Greeks flocked to the cause and much of the Peloponnese soon fell into rebel hands. A governing Greek Senate was set up, and a plump but shrewd clan chief called Petrobey Mavromihalis was voted its leader. In a romantic gesture towards the great days of Ancient Greece, Petrobey was proclaimed 'Commander-in-Chief of the Spartan forces'.

Meanwhile, the Patriarch's execution set off a series of tit-for-tat atrocities. The Greeks massacred forty thousand Turks in the Peloponnese and Greeks in Turkish cities were massacred in revenge. The Greek islands, especially the richest, Chios, suffered horribly with 25,000 Greeks slaughtered and 45,000 sold into slavery. This particular atrocity inspired the French artist Eugene Delacroix to paint the sensational *Scenes de Massacres de Scio* (now at the Louvre, Paris). Images of Christians dying at the hands of Muslims stirred a great outpouring of sympathy in Europe. Supporters of Greek Independence, called the Philhellenes, sent help from all over the world.

If you're on Chios
The Philip Argentis Museum, on the second floor of the Adamantios Korais Library, houses a fine copy of Delacroix's influential painting and the wonderful Nea Moni monastery nearby holds a gruesome collection of skulls from the massacre of 1822.

The Elgin Marbles

In the early years of the nineteenth century, the wealthy Earl of Elgin paid to have some of the marble statuary ripped from the ruined temples on the Acropolis in Athens. He said he was protecting them from harm and that the pagan images were about to be ground down for cement. The marbles were shipped to London. Despite Lord Elgin's good intentions, some minor damage was done while the statues were being ripped out and they suffered further after being kept in a damp London coal shed for ten years. They were eventually sold to the British Museum (at a loss).

Actually, Elgin may have been right. The marbles had been in danger throughout Turkish rule. The Turks used the Parthenon as a gunpowder store for years and, in 1686, a Venetian cannonball blew it up, which was why it was in such a poor condition when Lord Elgin first saw it. In 1822, after the marbles had been moved to England and during a siege of Athens by Greek rebels trying to regain control of the city, the Greeks themselves fired exploding mortars at the Acropolis where their Turkish enemies were holed up.

In 1981, the Greek actress Melina Merkouri began a campaign to get the marbles back. They are still in the British Museum, and still a bone of contention between the English and the Greeks.

Philhellenes

The Philhellenes (from the Greek, meaning 'lovers of Greece') were a mixed bunch. Some were soldiers at a loose end after the Napoleonic Wars, others were out for adventure, or the chance to kill a few Turks. They tended to be free spirits. Among them were a Spanish girl dressed as a man and a crazed German potter who wanted to start a china factory. Most were romantics who dreamed of the ideals and heroes of Ancient Greece. This meant that, on arriving in Greece, reality tended to let them down. The Greek guerrilla bands were clansmen, local people who fought in their own time-honoured and very ruthless ways. They showed few of the supposed characteristics of the ancient Greeks and they bristled like porcupines with pistols, daggers and swords. They in their turn were singularly unimpressed by most of the Philhellenes. The two groups were so different that a 'westernised' Greek revolutionary leader, Alexandros Mavrokordatos, had to set up a special 'Battalion of Philhellenes' to accommodate them. Sadly, this little army was almost wiped out at the Battle of Peta in 1822, after the treachery of a rival Greek band.

A portly poet

The English poet, Lord George Gordon Byron, is the most famous of the Philhellenes. The superstar of his age, he was famous for poetry, womanising and his love of Greece. When the War of Independence started, he was in Italy having fled England following scandalous accusations of an affair with his half-sister. In Italy he met up with Alexandros Mavrokordatos who was campaigning for support for the Greek cause. Byron raised money from sympathisers in England and contributed a fair proportion of his own wealth. He then sailed to Greece with money and arms and anchored at Kefallonia while he made up his mind how best to proceed.

If you're in Kefallonia
Lord Byron stayed for several months in the pretty inland village of Metaxata, in the district of Levathos, before moving to Mesolongi, his last location. It was in Metaxata that he wrote his famous poem, *Don Juan*. There is a bust of him in the village square.

While he was anchored, a plea for help came from Mavrokordatos who by then had returned to take part in the struggle. This dome-headed, bespectacled Greek was an unlikely-looking freedom fighter but he was in charge of Greek defences at the crucial port of Mesolongi. Byron sailed to join him - and not a moment too soon. By late 1823, the War of Independence was faltering. The freedom fighters needed a believable figure to rally round and they needed arms and hard cash. When the portly, scarlet-uniformed Lord Byron stepped ashore at Mesolongi on January 25, 1824, it was to a fanfare of martial music, excited cheers and the rattle of carbines. The Greeks had a new hero.

But not for long. In early April, Byron foolishly went for a horse-ride in the rain, caught a chill and became terribly ill. Blood-sucking leeches were applied, making him much worse, and he died a few days later. He'd given at least £20,000 to the cause, perhaps a million pounds in today's money. Despite not losing his life in heroic battle, Byron is still close to Greek hearts.

If you're in Mesolongi
Visit the Garden of Heroes. Byron's heart is buried under his statue.

The Battle of the Mounds

From 1821, when the Greek Revolt started, until early in 1822, Turkish forces were distracted by their fight with the upstart Albanian, Ali Pasha. But, on 5 February of that year, Ali Pasha was shot while cowering in the attic of a monastery near Ioannina. Musket balls from the Sultan's troops came crashing up through the floorboards below, killing him instantly. His head was put on display in Constantinople and Sultan Mahmud II could now turn his attention on the Greek rebels.

The first Turkish thrust after the death of Ali Pasha was crushed by a pony-tailed, hook-nosed bandit chief called Theodoros Kolokotronnis. The second was stopped by the resourceful Mavrokordatos at Mesolongi. Over the next seven years, the War came and went as town after town was captured and retaken by both sides.

Mesolongi bravely fought off three sieges and came to represent the defiance of a nation. It even managed to put out a newspaper, run by a dedicated Swiss Philhellene, Johann Meyer. The town was surrounded by towers and earth walls so it was hard for the Turks to break in. They built higher earth mounds to fire down onto the Greek side. Then more earth was added to form an embankment pushing into the Greek defences. But then the Greeks rebuilt their wall to surround the encroachment so that the attacking Turks were now the ones under siege. The next Turkish action in this amazing earthmoving contest was to build an even higher mound. The Greeks promptly

dug a tunnel underneath and blew it up with gunpowder. At night, gangs of Greek men, women and children would rush out, dig up and take away sections of the Turkish earthworks. The joke spread round Greece: 'What are our people in Mesolongi doing?': 'They're stealing earth!'

If you're in the Peloponnese

The Turks came under siege too, notably at Monemvasia, known as the 'Gibraltar of Greece', a high, rocky island which split off from the mainland after an earthquake in AD 375. In 1821, the starving Turkish garrison held out against their Greek besiegers for five months before the horrors of cannibalism forced them to hand over the fortress's keys.

Navarino

But all was not well. The idea of nationhood was alien to most Greek clansmen. Even people from the next valley were often treated like enemy foreigners. Feuding was a way of life. Robbery too - clan chiefs were called 'Klefts', literally 'thieves'. Even those lucky enough to escape the massacres on Chios and make it to the mainland were mugged as they came ashore.

In 1823, as soon as the immediate threat from the Turks seemed to be over, splits developed between the various Greek rebel groups. A practical soldier called Ioannis Makriyannis became infuriated by the squabbling:

I took an oath to fight Turks, not Greeks.

He was right to be angry. If the rebels carried on like this they were going to snatch defeat from the jaws of victory. By autumn 1824, with Byron dead and a new, reorganised

Turkish army on the march in the north, they were in deep trouble. Worse still, in the south the Sultan's powerful Egyptian ally, Ibrahim Pasha, was on his way with a fleet of ships. Ibrahim Pasha's Egyptians landed near Navarino in early 1825. By the end of the year, the Peloponnese was back under Turkish control while, in the north, starved-out Mesolongi finally fell, a devastating blow to Greek morale.

The Egyptian leader, Ibrahim Pasha, had been promised Greece as his own little kingdom if he could conquer the rebels. Once again, not that the Greeks were angels, the sheer brutality of their enemies came to their aid. Ibrahim Pasha proposed a mass eviction of the troublesome Greeks, to be replaced with his own Egyptian serfs - 'barbarisation' in the words of the day. His plan stirred up a hornet's nest in the capitals of Europe.

Britain, the superpower of the age, saw the Mediterranean as part of her domain and Ibrahim Pasha's so-called 'barbarisation' scheme was an insult to civilisation from the viewpoint of London liberals. Others thought so too. In July 1827, the Great Powers (Britain, France and Russia) signed the Treaty of London, in effect a demand for the Ottoman government to end the war and a guarantee of self-rule for Greece. It was time to send in the gunboats.

A joint European fleet was despatched forthwith. On arrival, it penned Ibrahim Pasha's ships in Navarino Bay. Strangely, the Egyptian ships carried French advisers hired to improve the Pasha's navy. Their last job was to arrange the blockaded fleet in a defensive formation before joining their countrymen on the French ships. Ibrahim's fleet, trapped as it was, didn't stand a chance. In four hours of vicious fighting on 20 October 1827, sixty of his eighty-nine ships were sunk against an incredible none on the allied side.

Navarino was a turning point in history, the last great battle of the age of sail and the battle that guaranteed Greek independence.

> **If you're in Pylos (old Navarino)**
> The Peloponnese port of Pylos has an obelisk in the town square commemorating the allied admirals' victory. The nearby castle of Niokastro (now an interesting museum) overlooks the siteof the Battle in the cramped Navarino Bay.

Kapodistrias comes - and goes
On 18 January 1828, the Phanariot Ioannis Kapodistrias, first President of Greece, set foot on Greek soil at Nafplion. Typically, the Greeks were still fighting amongst themselves. Rival commanders were bombarding each other from Nafplion's two fortresses even as the President's ship landed.

A slight, delicate-featured man, Kapodistrias's looks belied his strength of character. He set to work, banging Greek heads together until they saw sense. By September 1829 the last few Turks had left for home.

Most Greeks loved Kapodistrias, but his tough manner didn't go down well with the clan chiefs, the klefts, who didn't want to see the spoils of victory handed over to the politicians in Athens. Two clansmen, Georgios and

Konstantinos Mavromihalis, waited for Kapodistrias to arrive at church on Sunday 9 October 1831, then shot and stabbed him as he entered.

Top-hatted statesmen in distant London and Paris threw up their hands in frustration. Hadn't they just won the Battle of Navarino for the Greeks? Now they would have to step in once again.

If you're in Nafplion

One of the most attractive towns in Greece, Nafplion was originally a Venetian fortified port and became the capital of Greece for a brief period from 1829 to 1834. President Kapodistrias was assassinated near the church of Agios Spyridon.

THE FIRST TWO KINGS

... AND THE BIG IDEA

In Brief - early monarchy in Greece

1831	President Kapodistrias assassinated.
1833-62	Reign of King Otto.
1844	Ioannis Kolettis crystalises the *Megali Idea*.
1863	Start of reign of King George.
1864	Ionian Islands ceded to Greece.
1896	First modern Olympic Games.
1897	Major defeat in war with the Turks.
1913	King George assassinated.

Otto...or notto?

After President Kapodistrias' assassination in 1831, it became pretty clear that keeping a Greek-born head of state in power, or even alive for that matter, would be almost impossible if the quarrelsome Greeks were left to their own devices. Britain, France and Russia decided to install their own choice of leader. They looked around for someone young, biddable - and royal. They needed someone they could all agree on and lighted upon seventeen-year-old Otto, Prince of Bavaria, a fairly arbitrary choice but he seemed the most suitable candidate. A few discrete enquiries having established that the young prince was ready for the task, Otto packed his things, said goodbye to friends and lederhosen and set off to meet his destiny.

Young Otto, first King of Greece, was warmly welcomed when he arrived in Nafplion in early 1833 on board an armed British frigate, but he brought an awful lot of problems:

* Otto was accompanied by a retinue of 3,500 Bavarian troops and a Council of Regency, also Bavarian. Greeks asked themselves if they'd just swapped the Turks for a different bunch of foreign rulers.

* Otto was Roman Catholic; Greece was Greek Orthodox. This was hardly ideal.

* Otto was supposed to start a royal dynasty; sadly, he and his Queen, Amalia, didn't have any children.

All of these problems might have been overcome if Otto hadn't been such an arrogant young twerp. On top of this, he was slow to sort out the robber chieftains. For years there were bandit-infested no-go areas all over Greece. Eventually, the army became fed up with alternating aimlessness and being ordered about and in 1843, they threw Otto's advisers out of the country. Otto was forced to agree to a new sort of 'constitutional monarchy'. From now on, the Greeks were determined to have more say in how their country was run.

What's the Big Idea?
Otto's first choice of Prime Minister under the new rules was a veteran intriguer called Ioannis Kolettis. Kolettis had been a big player in the Independence struggle and, perhaps more impressively, before that he'd survived being the villainous Ali Pasha's doctor. Kolettis was a political schemer. He was brilliant at playing one faction off against another, often battering down the opposition with the trump card of Greek pride and growing nationalism. In a speech in 1844, he crystallised the *Megali Idea*, the 'Big Idea' of creating an expanded, greater Greece

to include all the Greeks and all Greek lands still outside the 1830 borders:

> *A Greek is not only someone who lives in this Kingdom, but also one who lives in Ioannina, in Thessaly, in Serres, in Adrianople, in Constantinople, in Trebizond, in Crete, in Samos - or in any place connected to Greek history or the Greek nation...*

This boiling obsession to make the *Megali Idea* a reality was the core Greek ambition for the next eighty years.

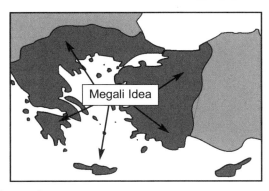

A measly end

Immediately after independence, land had been shared out among Greek peasants but the sharing had been botched. Most farms were too small, or on poor soil. Ordinary farmers just about scratched a living but one poor season could wipe them out. A few rich landowners got richer still at the expense of the others - and Otto got the blame. Grumbling revolts sprang up over the next few years, but it was the spectre of the unfulfilled *Megali Idea* that really led to Otto's downfall.

In 1854, the Crimean War broke out. In this war, Britain, France and Turkey resisted a Russian advance into Turkey from the north. Otto, himself inspired by the *Megali Idea*, decided to grab 'Greek' land from the Turks while they were busy fighting Russia. He sent bands of Greek brigands over the border into Turkish-held Epirus and Thessaly. It was a foolish move. Britain and France were now on the side of the Turks and they were hardly likely to support activity against their new ally. British and French forces stormed into the Greek port of Piraeus and threatened to occupy Athens itself. Otto had to back down and bring his men back. It was humiliation, pure and simple. By 1861, Otto was in deep trouble. Radical students even tried to assassinate Queen Amalia*.

Despite Otto's devious behaviour, Britain and France were unwilling to see the downfall of their Greek king. British envoy, Sir Henry Elliot, was sent to help Otto through his difficulties, but he might as well have saved himself the trouble. While passing through the Ionian Islands (held by the British since 1815), he discovered that the locals already thought that Otto was on his way out. They expected him to be replaced by Queen Victoria's son, Prince Alfred. Sir Henry met Otto three times and attempted to persuade him to change his policies, but his warnings fell on deaf ears - literally. The king was becoming hard of hearing and the meetings were mostly just shouting matches.

Eventually, it became clear, even to Otto, that his time had

---

*Dumpy Queen Amalia put even more weight on in later life. She died in 1875 of a heart attack, probably brought on by the shock of King Ludwig II rejecting her plans to be buried next to her husband. Ludwig ungraciously told her that she was too fat for the tomb.

come. He was deposed by the army in 1862 and left Greece as he had arrived, thirty years before, on a British warship. He retired to Bavaria where he died of measles in 1867.

Greece needed a new king.

A fishy story

Early one morning in April 1863, a seventeen-year-old naval cadet left his home in Copenhagen to go to school as usual. He strolled down towards the harbour, a slim, jaunty young man, daydreaming of adventures and a career in the navy. As usual, he carried his lunch with him, sardine sandwiches wrapped in newspaper to stop the oil from leaking. Glancing at the paper as he walked along, he was amazed to read his own name. As he read on, he was even more amazed - the powers that be had chosen him to be the new King of the Greeks!

Of course, the cadet was no ordinary sailor. His full name was Prince Christian William Ferdinand Adolphus George of Schleswig-Holstein-Sonderburg-Glucksburg, his father was next in line to the Danish throne and his sister, Princess Alexandra, had recently married the Prince of Wales, the future King Edward VII of England. He was in fact extremely royal, if in a minor sort of way.

Cadet William's promotion to king, as described in the newspaper, had its origins in what had seemed at the time like a casual conversation. After the wedding of his sister to the Prince of Wales, young William had got chatting with the British Prime Minister, Lord Palmerston.

Palmerston had asked him if he'd like to be 'King of Greece' but William had thought it was a joke. He'd laughed, his first thought being that as King of Greece, he wouldn't have to take the dreaded cadet school exams! 'I'd like nothing better,' he'd said.

But Palmerston had meant it. The British needed a new 'friendly' king in Greece to replace Otto. On Palmerston's recommendation, the Greek Assembly in Athens quickly voted for William to be their new king, the second time a foreign teenager had been chosen for the job. Palmerston threw in the Ionian Islands as a sort of wedding gift.

The new 'crown jewels' arrive

King William turned out to be much smarter than King Otto and he understand the importance of PR. From the moment he set foot on Greek soil, he tried hard to be as Greek as possible:

* Instead of 'William', he used his last name, George (more familiar in Greek). He grew a big, drooping manly moustache and quickly learned the language.

* George I's official title was to be 'King of the Hellenes' (the Greek name for themselves) rather than 'King of the Greeks' (the old Roman name).

* He arrived in Athens on his own yacht, the *Hellas*, not in a British warship.

* He promised that his children would be brought up in the Greek Orthodox faith, and he married a Orthodox sixteen-year-old Russian Duchess called Olga.

George was determined never to get too 'grand' for his subjects. For all his royal blood, the trappings of royalty never interested him much and, in any case, King Otto had taken the royal regalia with him to Bavaria. When some sceptic asked George, mockingly, where his crown was, George proudly answered that the Ionian Islands were the only jewels he'd brought*.

Canals with currants

In 1875, twelve years after his coronation and after various experiments in government, King George appointed Kharilaos Trikoupis, a shipping magnate and a so-called 'new man' to be Prime Minister. Trikoupis was from a London Greek merchant family and he spoke Greek with an English accent. King and Prime Minister were determined to modernise their country. They started work on a canal to cut through the isthmus of Corinth and King George himself dug the first, symbolic shovelful. The Corinth Canal opened in 1893 and, almost overnight, Piraeus became one of the Mediterranean's greatest ports.

> ### If you're near ancient Corinth
> The Roman emperor Nero first ordered work to begin on a Corinth canal some eighteen hundred years before work on the current canal was begun in 1882. His intention was to shorten the dangerous trip round the rocky southern shores of Greece. In the modern age of giant container ships the canal has become a bit obsolete, but it's fascinating to watch the smaller freighters and their tugboats negotiate the narrow channel.

In general though, Greece was frustratingly slow to respond to their modernising efforts and they were

*The Crown, Orb and Sceptre of the King of the Hellenes were eventually returned to Greece on December 20 1959 by Duke Albrecht of Bavaria. He thought it was the least he could do after the recent 'misunderstandings' between Greece and Germany (ie World War II).

starting from a very low base. In 1875, the country only had about 7,000 factory workers compared to the millions employed in Britain, France and Germany. It remained a mostly rural country, its main export being currants. Luckily, profits shot through the roof after 1858 when a greenfly-like pest, *Phylloxera vastatrix*, wiped out rival grape crops in other Mediterranean countries.

Even Trikoupis, new man though he was, was not immune to the *Megali Idea*. In 1875, the Serbs and Montenegrins started a fight with Turkey and Trikoupis couldn't resist the chance to join in and grab some land. Guerrilla warfare broke out in Epirus and Thessaly, parts of which were granted to the Greeks in 1881 at the end of this particular round of fighting. Importantly, the great symbol of Mount Olympus, home of the gods, was now part of Greece.

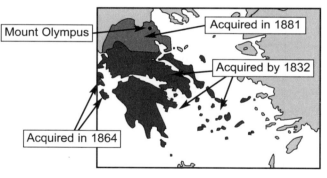

If you're in Greek Macedonia
The remote slopes of Mount Olympus, height 2,918 metres, make for excellent hiking country. There are Roman ruins and an excellent museum in the nearby town of Dion (a city once sacred to the ancient Macedonians). The museum contains a fascinating collection of objects excavated from the local temples.

Then disaster struck. A dramatic fall in the price of currants and the worldwide financial crisis of 1893 led to Greece defaulting on her huge foreign debts. Trikoupis's last job before leaving office in disgrace was to declare his country bankrupt.

The pig-headed push

For many years, Trikoupis's arch rival on the Athenian political scene had been a sabre-rattling politician called Theodoros Deliyannis. Deliyannis's main policy might best be described as pig-headed opposition to anything and everything Trikoupis stood for. Despite his adventure of 1875, Trikoupis generally had pushed for peace and economic growth; Deliyannis was obsessed with one idea - the *Megali Idea*.

Now the warlike Deliyannis swept to power and began to push the *Megali Idea* for all it was worth. In early 1897 he ordered Greek troops into Turkish-held Thessaly (yet again). The troops were disorganised and poorly led and they were comprehensively thrashed by superior Turkish forces. Greece slumped back on itself as a result and for years there were bitter recriminations. It was period of social decline and economic stagnation. From 1890 to 1920, Greece lost 500,000 of her best young people. They emigrated, chiefly to America.

The Games come home

Banned as a pagan abomination by the Christian Emperor Theodosius in 393 AD, by the late nineteenth century the ancient Olympic Games had been dead and buried for 1500 years. It took the efforts of an energetic Frenchman, Baron Pierre de Coubertin, to revive them. The Baron planned for the first modern Games to be held in Paris in 1900, but the newly formed International Olympic Committee, under its first President, Dimitrios Vikelas of Greece, couldn't wait that long. The first modern Olympics was held in Athens in 1896.

The Games were a brilliant success. The Greek team won ten events and came second in the medal table after the USA. But the most important victory was in the marathon, won by the local shepherd Spiridon Louis who ran barefoot, his compatriot Kharilaos Vassilakos coming in second. Such was the joy of the royal spectators in particular that two of King George's sons, Princes Constantine and George, ran down to accompany Louis over the last thousand yards.

If you're in Athens
The impressive, marble Kallimarmaro Stadium, in central Athens, was specially built for the revived Olympic Games of 1896 on the site of the ancient Panathenaic Stadium. It is an exact replica of a rebuilt stadium used for the Games of AD 144, shortly after the death of the Emperor Publius ('Pub the Builder') Hadrian.

Death in Thessaly

On the evening of 17 March 1913, two of George's sons, Princes Constantine, the elder, and Christopher, were attending an automatic writing séance in Ioannina. Séances were a bit of a craze at that time. After a long wait, the pencil began to jerk then suddenly flew across the paper. The scribbled spirit message promised glory for Constantine but signed off with the words 'DEATH' and 'TOMORROW'.

If you're in Salonika

Capital of the Roman province of Macedonia after 146 BC and held by the Turks from 1430 to 1912, Salonika is now Greece's second city. Although about half of the medieval city was destroyed by the Great Fire of 1912, much has been restored, including Greece's largest church, Agios Dimitrios. The Archeological and Folk Museums offer fascinating insights into life in Salonika through the ages.

Next day, George I, King of the Hellenes, was assassinated. Strangely, George himself may have felt a chilling premonition. Over lunch in Salonika on the day of his death, he told another son, Nicholas, that he was looking forward to retiring. Fifty years was plenty long enough to be king, he said. After lunch, he went for his customary stroll, unprotected except for an equerry and two gendarmes, a dangerous move in a city which had only been captured from the Turks a few months earlier.

As George passed a seedy café called the 'Pasha Liman', a shabbily dressed man pulled out a gun and shot him in the back, killing him instantly. The assassin, Alexandros Schinas, later gave a confused story about being angry because the King hadn't given him some money, but rumours soon spread that Schinas was a Bulgarian nationalist. Prince Nicholas, desperate to avoid a violent ethnic backlash from his countrymen, quickly declared the assassin to be Greek, a madman and probably drunk. Schinas himself gave no further explanation. He committed suicide two months later by jumping out of a cell window.

GREECE'S GREAT WAR

THE END OF THE IDEA

> ### In Brief - the First World War in Greece
>
> | | |
> |---|---|
> | 1909 | The Goudi coup. |
> | 1910-35 | Eleftherios Venizelos active. |
> | 1911-13 | Balkan wars. |
> | 1913 | King George assassinated, Constantine beomes king. |
> | 1915 | Ill-fated Dardanelles campaign. |
> | 1916 | National Schism begins. |
> | 1920 | King Alexander dies of a monkey bite. |
> | 1922 | Burning of Smyrna (Izmir). |
> | 1923 | Peak of population exchange. |

The Goudi coup

The warlike Delyannis's campaign in pursuit of the *Megali Idea* back in 1897 had been a political as well as a military disaster. In the grim years which followed, organised political life almost came to a standstill. Some people blamed the army for what had gone wrong but the army leaders in their turn blamed the politicians. They claimed that they hadn't been given enough money to train and equip the troops. A mood of irritable discontent spread among the officer corps and a secret society, called the Military League, grew up, demanding a say in how the country was run. In September 1909, the soldiers launched a coup from the main barracks at Goudi and forced the government from office.

This coup was rather futile and it's only important for what came after. The leaders of the coup, Colonels

Nikolaos Zorbas and Theodoras Pangolos, had no idea how to run the economy and before long, foreign bankers threatened to call in their debts, which would have caused financial melt-down. To placate the bankers, the colonels drafted in someone who knew what he was about.

Enter the crafty, charismatic Cretan, Eleftherios Venizelos, George I's last prime minister and a very remarkable man.

'All Cretans are liars'

Back in the sixth century BC, the Cretan poet Epimenides is supposed to have come up with a paradox: if he says 'All Cretans are liars', should you believe him or not? This was meant as an interesting brain teaser, though throughout the ancient world Cretans did have a reputation for deviousness. A similar paradox is that of the lawyer who says 'All lawyers are liars'. Eleftherios Venizelos was both a Cretan and a lawyer!

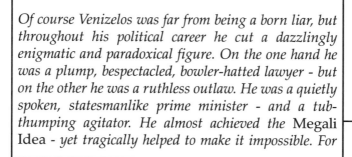

Of course Venizelos was far from being a born liar, but throughout his political career he cut a dazzlingly enigmatic and paradoxical figure. On the one hand he was a plump, bespectacled, bowler-hatted lawyer - but on the other he was a ruthless outlaw. He was a quietly spoken, statesmanlike prime minister - and a tub-thumping agitator. He almost achieved the **Megali Idea** *- yet tragically helped to make it impossible. For*

↑

years he was both the most loved and the most hated man in Greece.

When Venizelos entered Cretan politics in 1889, the island of Crete was still part of the Ottoman Empire but its mostly Greek population wanted union, or enosis, *with Greece. When King George's second son, Prince George, became High Commissioner of Crete in 1898, the islanders rejoiced: surely* enosis *could only be a matter of time? But years passed and still nothing happened. In 1905, the exasperated Venizelos led a band of rebels into the hills and declared Crete's* enosis *with Greece. The Great Powers sent in the gunboats to restore order and Venizelos had to give in, but not before he'd become a Greek national hero.*

Battles in the Balkans

Venizelos was a godsend for Greece. Between 1910 and 1912, he poured money into reorganising and re-equipping the army and put forward hundreds of new laws to heal the divisions that had plagued the country for years.

Then in 1911, the Italians and the Turks went to war in the Balkans and Venizelos threw his revamped army into the fray. This was the First Balkan War when Greece joined forces with Serbia, Montenegro and Bulgaria to throw the Turks out of the Balkans once and for all. The short Second Balkan War of 1913 was an argument over the spoils, Greece and Serbia on one side and Bulgaria on the other. For Greece, the main outcome of these wars was the capture of Crete, Samos and other islands, as well as vast areas of Epirus, Macedonia and Thessaly. The outcome for King George was his assassination in newly conquered

Salonika in 1913, and the outcome for Prince Constantine was that he became king in place of his father.

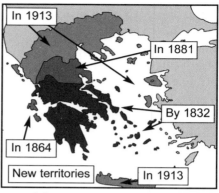

As for Venizelos, the Greek public elevated him to almost god-like status.

'...we should remain neutral.'

When the First World War broke out in 1914, Venizelos was sure that the *Triple Entente* (Britain, France and Russia) would win. To ensure a share in the future spoils, Greeks would need to do their bit on the winning side. He made a secret deal with the British: Venizelos would hand over part of Thrace to the Bulgarians to keep them out of the War and in return, when peace came, Greece would receive 'important territorial concessions on the coast of Asia Minor'.

Consumed with dreams of the *Megali Idea*, Venizelos thought this was a pretty smart deal but King Constantine did not. To throw away the territory they'd only just won in exchange for vague promises seemed to him shockingly irresponsible. In any case, he'd been trained by the German army and had a deep respect for the German war machine. Maybe the Germans would win? To make matters worse, he had family on both sides. His wife, Sofia, was Kaiser Wilhelm of Germany's sister, and King George V of Britain was his cousin. As he confided early on to his brother, Prince Nicholas,

> *We are Greeks, and the interests of Greece must come first...it is imperative that we should remain neutral.*

Venizelos however condemned the king's inaction as blatant cowardice, or worse - treachery. Popular rumour had long held that Constantine was secretly in league with the Germans. When British and Commonwealth troops attacked the Turks in the Dardanelles in February 1915. Venizelos planned to join in but Constantine, to Venizelos's intense annoyance, cautiously held back the Greek army. Venizelos fumed over what he saw as royal interference in government affairs, but Constantine was right. The Dardanelles offensive turned out to be a massive failure - and Bulgaria invaded Serbia anyway.

The vicious argument between Venizelos and the King sparked off what became known as the 'National Schism'. Greece was split right down the middle, with, in effect, two governments, one run by the king and one run by Venizelos.

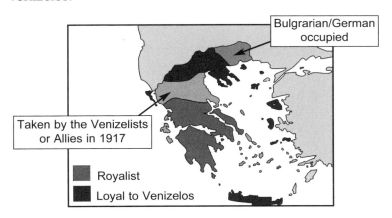

The physical split took place in August 1916, when pro-Venizelos army officers staged a coup in Salonika. Venizelos joined them and set up an alternative government, and French and British forces were at last made welcome in Greece. In the south, their ships blockaded Piraeus. Starvation set in and normal life in

Athens became impossible. The beaten Constantine had no choice but to abdicate in favour of his son, Alexander. He went into exile in Switzerland and Venizelos returned to power in Athens.

Polly gone

When the triumphant Venizelists returned to Athens in 1917, they were determined to stamp out support for the exiled King Constantine. Among other measures, it became illegal to sing The Son of the Eagle, *a song composed to honour Constantine's victories in the Balkan Wars. An armed patrol once broke into a house when they heard the familiar melody, only to find a little old lady listening to her pet parrot squawking the tune. They promptly wrung the bird's neck and marched out again without a word.*

Monkey business

Sadly, King Alexander wasn't on the throne for long. On 2 October 1920, he visited the vineyard keeper's house in the grounds of Tatoi, a large royal retreat near Athens. Two pet monkeys were scampering about in the garden as the king approached with his dog, Fritz. Alexander had rescued Fritz from a Bulgarian trench years earlier and was devoted to him. Suddenly, one of the monkeys leapt chattering and screaming onto the dog's back and began frenziedly scratching and biting. As Alexander tried to break up the fight, the second monkey attacked him, leaving deep wounds on his legs and stomach.

At first Alexander was only concerned that the doctors keep the absurd, embarrassing details of the incident a secret. But later that evening a fever set in and by the following morning his condition was so serious that medical experts from around Europe were called to the palace. But there was nothing they could do. Septicaemia was followed quickly by jaundice, pneumonia and dysentery. Alexander lasted an agonisingly painful three more weeks, but died on 25 October.

If you're in Athens

The royal retreat at Tatoi to the north of Athens is now publically owned and can be visited free of charge. Its tree-lined lanes and scattered redundant buildings (there's even a private, royal police station) have an air of melancholic but romantic abandonment.

Time to carve

For two years after the First World War, Venizelos haunted the diplomatic corridors of Versailles and London, bustling from one meeting to another, forever angling for fulfilment of the *Megali Idea*. But now that the war was over, Britain and France were wary of the growing power of newly communist Russia. They had no interest in helping the Greeks to carve themselves slices of Turkey, a nation which was useful for holding back the Russian hordes. The promised land would have to be captured by the Greeks on their own.

But by 1920, despite Venizelos's plots and plans, the Greek people were tired of war, tired even of Venizelos. They wanted peace. Moreover, after King Alexander's strange death, they wanted 'good old' King Constantine back from exile in Switzerland. During the autumn of that year assassins attempted to murder Venizelos while he was in Paris. His wounds meant that he wasn't fit for the campaign trail that November and he lost the general election. The new government promptly arranged a referendum on whether Constantine should be restored to the throne. Constantine came back the following year - and Venizelos went into voluntary exile in France.

But even without Venizelos, the *Megali Idea* had an unstoppable life of its own. Both King Constantine and his new government wanted the 'important territorial concessions on the coast of Asia Minor' that the Entente powers had promised back in 1915.

Turkey was on the menu again.

The end of the dream

Greek troops had occupied the Turkish port of Smyrna (Izmir) in May 1919, soon after the end of the war. They were waiting for orders to advance. Now, as rumours of a Greek advance began to spread, hordes of Asian Greeks from inland Turkey surged towards the coast in fear of Turkish reprisals. Turks fled in the other direction. There were dreadful atrocities on both sides.

The Greeks pushed inland. All went well at first, but as the Turks retreated, the Greek supply lines became more and more stretched. By August 1922, the Turkish army leader, Mustapha Kemal, calculated that the Greeks had been dragged far enough into Turkey. His counter-attack was a devastating move. By the middle of September, the Turks had burst through the Greek lines and marched into Smyrna. There they set about taking their revenge. As the city burned, Greek and Armenian refugees thronged the waterfront, hopelessly seeking escape. Tens of thousands died horrible deaths.

The *Megali Idea* died with them in the fires of Smyrna.

Population exchange

A month after the Smyrna disaster, two Venizelist army officers, Nikolaos Plastiras and Stilianos Gonatos, launched a coup against Constantine's government. In July 1923, having struggled with the appalling aftermath of Smyrna for several months, the coup leaders asked Venizelos to return from his self-imposed exile in France. Venizelos did what he could but the disaster had taken on a life of its own. People, both Greeks and Turks, were scrambling 'home', moving in vast uncontrollable hordes through the porous borders and across the treacherous Aegean Sea. One eyewitness later wrote:

> ...the ships were buffeted about for several days at sea before their wretched human cargoes could be brought to land. Typhoid and smallpox swept through the ships. Lice infested everyone. Babies were born on board. Men and women went insane. Some leapt overboard to end their miseries in the sea; those who survived were landed without shelter upon the open beach, loaded with filth, racked by fever, without blankets or even warm clothing, without food and without money.

Few of either race cared to stay and be 'ethnically cleansed', as the modern phrase has it. Between 1913 and 1939, perhaps 560,000 Turks left Europe for Asia Minor and about 1,360,000 Greeks moved in the opposite direction.

With hardly anyone left to liberate, the *Megali Idea* had run its course.

There was little left to do but to rubber-stamp the unofficial migration. The Treaty of Lausanne, 24 July 1923, oversaw one of the largest exchanges of populations ever seen. For Greece, there was a whole new set of problems to sort out. Somehow, this new population, as well as the wartime refugees, had to be housed, fed, employed and made 'Greek'. It wasn't going to be easy.

The Rambling Republic

Greece between the Wars

In Brief - the first Greek Republic

1923	George II deposed.
1924	Monarchy abolished.
1924-35	Series of elected governments.
1928	Venizelos invited back from exile.
	(Start of 'Second Golden Age.')
1935	Return of George II from exile.
1936-41	Dictatorship of Ioannis Metaxas.

Boxing clever

The Revolutionary Committee looked round for scapegoats for the 1922 defeat. As well as inviting Venizelos back from exile, they forced King Constantine to abdicate (again), and had six members of his government executed by firing squad. Most of the royal family had already fled the country, but Constantine's brother, Prince Andrew, was tricked into returning. For his 'failures' while commanding Greek troops in Turkey he was tried and found guilty of treason, a capital crime. Fortunately, his British cousin, King George V, intervened and the death sentence was reduced to exile. Safely on board the British Navy cruiser *Calypso*, Andrew collected his family from Corfu and sailed for Rome. The frantic dash for safety meant that the family had to leave behind their youngest member's cot. Little Philip, the future Duke of Edinburgh, made his first major overseas journey in a converted orange box.

The royal family were just glad to have escaped. The *Calypso's* captain later recalled that they were wonderful company and that:

...they were rather amusing about being exiled, for they so frequently are!

If you're in Corfu

The British-built Mon Repos Villa was King George and his family's summer retreat and was Prince Philip's birthplace. The Villa and its extensive, beautifully kept gardens are open every day during the summer.

Exiled to Sicily this time, King Constantine lost the will to continue. He had been permanently ill since a botched operation to cure pleurisy in 1915. A patriot to the last, he died (January 1923) clutching to his chest a leather pouch of Greek soil. His eldest son, George, briefly became King George II, but his reign ended less than a year later after he foolishly got involved in a counter-coup plot. The plot was exposed, George II was deposed (December 1923) and went into exile, this time to Romania. In March 1924 the Revolutionary Committee abolished the Greek monarchy. It seemed that Greece's short, precarious flirtation with monarchy was over.

Royalty in exile

Europe in the 1920s was awash with the shabby genteel flotsam and jetsam of dispossessed royalty. From Broadstairs to Bucharest, refugee kings, queens, dowagers and duchesses traipsed, crowns in hand, from one gracious handout to the next. For a while, ex-King George II lived with his wife Elisabeth in her native Romania, but he grew tired of her love affairs and the sickly opulence of the Cotroceni Palace. He was more often to be found touring the royal retreats of Europe, keeping up with his vast extended family. London was particularly welcoming to George, lending as he did a spicy cachet to fashionable Mayfair dinner parties.

George and his brother Paul (next in line to the throne) never lost their ambition to go home to Greece one day, even if only as ordinary citizens. Paul's opportunity came first, in 1930, when he met a yacht owner who offered him a trip to the Greek Islands, posing as a deck hand. The young, homesick prince was tired of his rootless life and he leapt at the chance. Under a false name, Prince Paul was smuggled ashore near Athens, and for one glorious day he wandered the familiar gardens and dust-sheeted rooms of the beloved royal retreat at Tatoi.

Meanwhile, back in Greece

There were huge cultural differences between the 'old' Greeks and the 'new' Greek refugees from Turkey and other parts of the former Ottoman Empire following the population exchanges of 1913-39. The old Greeks laughed at the 'new' Greeks' funny Turkish food. For their part, many of the new Greeks came from sophisticated Turkish cities and looked down on the uncouth ways of old Greece. Many were educated professionals or had been rich landowners before being evacuated. Furthermore, the two groups often couldn't understand each other. The refugees from Turkey often only spoke Turkish. Greek speakers from the shores of the Black Sea arrived with a variety of baffling dialects.

Greece just didn't have the resources, the housing, money, jobs and hospitals to cope with the influx. Massive shanty towns grew up around Salonika and Athens. The *Megali Idea* had been a dream of expanding into Asia Minor and nobody had expected waves of 'foreign' Greeks to end up on their own doorstep. The newcomers were met with growing resentment and hostility. There were clashes between the natives and the refugees and, unsurprisingly, these struggles had their effect on Greek politics. The Greek Republic tottered from one crisis to another. Between 1924 and 1935, there were twenty-three elected governments and at least thirteen coups.

Something had to be done.

Venizelos (again)
After living abroad for six years, Venizelos was recalled by massive popular demand in elections in 1928. For the next four years he pushed through cheap loans to poor farmers, built houses to replace the shanties and started new schools to educate the 'new' children.

Things looked good for once, but Venizelos's 'Second Golden Age' was sadly short-lived. In trying to bind together all the people of Greece he had to clamp down hard on dissenters, especially people on the political extremes, such as monarchists or communists. Then came the Great Depression of the 1930s. Demand for Greek shipping fell and for the Greek 'luxury' goods: olive oil, currants and tobacco. Thousands were thrown out of work, Venizelos's glitter began to fade and he lost the 1932 elections to the monarchist Populist Party.

Next year, summer 1933, Venizelos escaped miraculously unharmed from his bullet-riddled car after yet another failed assassination attempt, amazingly, the eleventh of his long political career. Perhaps thinking himself indestructible, he gambled all on another coup in 1935, but it failed and he had to flee into exile, this time for the last time. He died in France the following year.

If you're in Crete
The Packard car, the bloodstained clothes from the 1920 attempt and other Venizelos memorabilia are on show at the Venizelos Museum at his house in Chalepa near Chania.

The return of the King

The monarchist Populist Party was just that, monarchist. They asked George II to come back, although George insisted on a referendum first to make sure that he'd really be welcome. Pro-Royalist fixers arranged a thumping 97% vote in his favour. The usual cheering, flag-waving crowds turned out to greet him when he stepped back on Greek soil (November 1935). From the monarchist point of view it all seemed to be good to be true. And it was.

The curse of the Greek monarchs struck almost immediately in the form of the sudden (and insanely unlikely) natural deaths in early 1936 of the top four senior Greek politicians. At a stroke, George had nobody with enough political clout to form a government. In desperation, he turned to an old friend by the name of Ioannis Metaxas.

First Peasant

Metaxas cut a rather ridiculous figure. Small, dumpy and short sighted, he looked more like somebody's favourite uncle from the country than a dictator. Indeed, he styled himself 'First Peasant' or 'National Father'. Some peasant. He even banned the Boy Scouts to stop it rivalling his own 'Youth Movement'.

Metaxas gave his new government the grandiose title of 'Regime of the Fourth of August 1936'. It was his version of the fascist dictatorships spreading through Europe, although he was no Hitler. Metaxas had no party and almost no popular support, not that he was the least interested in being popular. He had work to do, and work he did, often fifteen hours a day without so much as sandwich. Strikes were banned, the press was straitjacketed and secret police were everywhere. His frighteningly efficient Minister for Public Order, Konstantinos Maniadakis, was prepared to stoop to torture when the need arose and set up a fake underground 'communist party' to lure the lefties that his network of informers missed.

Metaxas' regime was unpleasant, but it got results. It improved pay and conditions for workers, organised loans and drainage projects to bring more land into use and revamped the inefficient civil service. If Metaxas had had a political organisation, it would have been called the 'Sensible Party'.

Peasant in pyjamas

The 'First Peasant' was first and foremost a soldier, and a very good one, if no longer young. He was one of the few people who could take credit from that distant, disastrous 1897 campaign when Greek troops had unsuccessfully invaded Turkish-held Thessaly. Greece being surrounded by enemies, he knew that it was vital that her army should be always at the ready. The diminutive dictator threw himself into the task of bringing it to fighting fitness, and only just in time.

In 1939, the fascist Benito Mussolini's Italian troops took over Albania and camped on the Greek border. At three o'clock in the morning on 28 October 1940, the Italian ambassador knocked on Metaxas's door and delivered an ultimatum: let the Italian army occupy strategic points on Greek soil or Italian troops would invade in three hours' time. Metaxas, a stubborn, proud little man, stood defiant in his pyjamas and uttered the Greek for 'No': *'Ochi!'*

The 'First Peasant' was suddenly, truly the 'National Father', a hero at last, his defiant stance sparking the embers of national fervour. The Italians attacked but Mussolini's hopes for quick and easy pickings in Greece were dashed. The Greeks swept westward and threw the overconfident Italians back into Albania. For a few heady weeks, it even looked as though the *Megali Idea* was reborn and that 100,000 Albanian Greeks would be welcomed the fold.

But a hard winter set in. The campaign stuttered to a halt and Ioannis Metaxas, visibly ageing and racked with illness from the strain of command, died in January 1941.

It was going to be a long war.

THEIR DARKEST HOUR
WAR AND CIVIL WAR

In Brief - the Second World War and after
1941   Death of Ioannis Metaxas.
1941   British soldiers arrive in Greece.
1941   Start of German occupation of Greece.
1943-9   Greek Civil War.
1947   Dodecanese Islands ceded to Greece.

The fall of Greece

World War II broke out in Europe in 1939. By the end of 1940, the wartime allies, Britain and Greece, stood alone against the might of Germany and Italy. Metaxas cautiously turned down Winston Churchill's offer to send British troops beef up Greek defences but when he died, at the end of January, his successor, Alexandros Koryzis, leapt at the chance. Two months later, 63,000 British and Commonwealth soldiers were on Greek soil.

The German response was swift and overwhelming, as Metaxas had rightly guessed. That April, most of the disorganised Greco-British force gave up almost without a fight. The allies were forced south in a ragged retreat and Koryzis shot himself when he heard the news. The Germans swept into Athens and the German SS fell gleefully on Maniadakis' old secret police files. Mass arrests of communists and Venizelists soon followed.

George II and some 27,000 men fled mainland Greece to make a stand on Crete, but the Germans were unstoppable. In May, the Cretan airfields were blitzed by the Luftwaffe and a devastating German paratroop campaign followed. The allies and the islanders put up a courageous fight but, by early June, Crete was lost. The king and the remnants of his government fled into exile, first to England, then to Egypt.

Partisans on patrol

Meanwhile, thousands of volunteers fled to the hills to fight the German occupation. The mountains of Greece have always been ideal for launching smash and grab raids on invaders and now tough guerrilla resistance fighters, called *andartes*, settled into the old secret boltholes, sometimes sacred caves from ancient times known only to local shepherds. There were women guerrillas, too, the famous bandoliered *andartisses*. By 1943, resistance groups were running small airfields to bring in supplies and British agents.

The volunteers joined various groups depending on their political preferences. Most important were the communist National People's Liberation Army (ELAS) and right wing groups such as the National Republican Greek Army (EDES) and the fascist 'X' group, run by the Cypriot, Georgios Grivas. Unfortunately, these groups spent as much time fighting each other as they did fighting the Germans and Italians. Grivas even collaborated with the enemy when it suited him.

Those Greeks who weren't in the hills had to endure life under more obvious military occupation. The country was split up between the occupying forces. Things were relatively relaxed in the Italian zone, but in the German zone the exploits of the resistance fighters brought down terrible reprisals. In 1943 the Nazis ordered that fifty Greek civilians would be shot for every German soldier killed. Whole villages were massacred. But that didn't stop the guerrillas. Every reprisal was another reason to keep on fighting. The Bulgarian-occupied zone was tough too. Ethnic hatred between Greeks and Bulgars forced 100,000 Greeks to flee from Thrace.

Salonika took the brunt of ethnic terror. At least 50,000 Salonikan Jews were sent to the German death camp at Auschwitz. More deadly still was the German policy of crushing resistance by siphoning off food for their war effort. This brought about another 200,000 deaths from starvation.

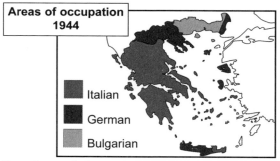

Areas of occupation 1944

Italian

German

Bulgarian

Civil War: Round One

In April 1943 while the war was still at its height, Winston Churchill ordered that only monarchist partisans would get weapons from Britain. From then on, the bulk of British assistance went to the previously Republican Greek Army of the EDES. This was because the EDES, run by a fat, pop-eyed drunk called Napoleon Zervas, quickly turned royalist when he heard about Churchill's deal. But though deprived of weapons by Churchill, the communist ELAS made up for it from other sources. After the Italians surrendered that September, large quantities of Italian guns and ammo fell into communist hands. Many of the thousands of Italian soldiers who had been left stranded in Greece by their government were massacred.

Now that the occupiers were on the back foot, the various resistance groups turned their guns on each other in earnest. There was a savage civil war, the main actors being the communist ELAS and the newly royalist EDES. The communists were better organised and, by February 1944, most of Greece was under their control. A communist government ruled 'Free Greece' almost as though peace had already arrived.

The Greek garage sale

World War II was moving into its final stages. Unknown to the Greeks, in October 1944, Churchill and the Russian leader Stalin came up with a secret 'percentages' deal over post-war spheres of influence. Churchill suggested to Stalin, almost casually, like someone haggling over bric-a-brac at a garage sale:

…So far as Britain and Russia are concerned, how would it do for you to have ninety per cent predominance in Romania, for us to have ninety per cent of the say in Greece, and go fifty-fifty about Yugoslavia?

Civil War: Round Two

In early October 1944, Germany started pulling its troops out of Greece so as to shore up its crumbling defences in the north. The Greek partisans forgot their differences for a few weeks and fell on the hated occupiers, slaughtering them in their thousands as they retreated.

For Greece it was the end of World War II, but not, however, the end of the Civil War. Led by the British, the Allies helped to install an anti-communist Prime Minister, Georgios Papandreou, in Athens. The communists, who controlled much of the country, refused to give up their weapons without a proper power sharing agreement. A demonstration of their supporters and other left-wingers in Athens turned ugly and street fighting broke out between British troops and the ELAS. By mid-January 1945, 11,000 people had died and central Athens was in ruins. Eventually, at a meeting at Varkiza, the ELAS promised to give up its weapons in exchange for amnesty and punishment for wartime collaborators such as Grivas.

There was fat hope of that.

Civil War: The Third Round

The promises of the anti-communists at Varkiza were worthless. A reign of terror began, and, far from being punished, Georgios Grivas's fascist 'X' group went on a rampage. Communists were 'disappeared', tortured or locked up. Many fled into the mountains, where their leader, Markos Vafiadis, set up the communist Democratic Army of Greece (DAG). The DAG armed themselves with guns smuggled in from fellow communists in neighbouring Yugoslavia and, to start with, things went well for them. But, in March 1947, everything fell apart. Britain pulled out of Greece and the Americans took over. American money to the tune of $1.25 billion was poured into the Greek economy and into the Greek National Army.

The DAG was outnumbered and out-resourced. The communists began to press-gang villagers into their ranks and children were abducted to be sent abroad for brainwashing in communist ideology. This was uncomfortably like a return to the bad old days of the *devirshme*, the 'child tax' during Turkish rule, and nothing was more likely to annoy ordinary Greeks. Civil war raged more fiercely than ever. Dreadful atrocities were committed by both sides as they passed to and fro through mountain villages. Newspapers carried photographs of bounty hunters holding up severed heads. It was Greece's darkest hour.

Finally, in January 1949, frustrated by the lack of progress by communist forces, a hard-line communist leader by the name of Nikos Zakhariadis seized command of the DAG. Zakhariadis was a refugee from Greek Turkey who had been imprisoned by Metaxas and was a survivor of the German concentration camp at Dachau. He was a very tough nut, but his communist army was doomed, regardless. Under pressure from Stalin, Yugoslavia stopped sending weapons to the DAG and closed the border in 1949. After a last, devastating defeat in the Grammos Mountains, the remnants of the DAG fled into exile in Albania.

The Civil War was over.

'THEY WILL STRIKE TONIGHT'
THE CRACKPOT COLONELS

In Brief - Rule of the Colonels	
1964	King Paul dies, Constantine II takes over.
1967	The Colonels' Coup, Constantine goes into exile.
1973	Colonel Papadopoulos becomes lifetime president.
1974	Monarchy abolished.
1974	Colonels' regime collapses

Party time

George II had returned to Greece in 1946, his third attempt at sitting on the throne, but died of a heart attack on April Fool's Day 1947. Out of the twenty-four years he'd been king, he'd spent just seven in Greece and all under military dictatorship at that. The Greek people hadn't had much of a chance to get to know him. The new king, George's younger brother Paul, and his young wife Frederika wanted their reign to be different.

King Paul was a handsome navy captain, Frederika was intelligent, bubbly, loved practical jokes and was blessed with the stunning looks of a Hollywood film star, and they both knew the value of a photo opportunity. One effective piece of propaganda showed them being carried shoulder-high by grinning 'reformed' communists on the infamous prison island of Makronisos.

Paul and Frederika loved parties, big ones preferably. In the summer of 1954 they invited over a hundred members of the royal families of twenty nations to join them on a 'Cruise of Kings' aboard the luxury liner, SS *Agamemnon*. On board, their daughter Princess Sophia met the exiled Prince Juan Carlos of Spain, both of them then aged sixteen. The two young royals were married eight years later and in 1975 became King and Queen of Spain. This glamorous holiday cruise is credited with kick-starting the post-war Mediterranean cruise industry as well as the boom in mass tourism in Greece.

The 'Colonels' Coup

Not everybody in Orthodox, male-dominated Greece liked Queen Frederika. Some called her 'Friki', meaning 'the horrible one'. She interfered too much in politics, they said, especially after her husband died suddenly in February 1964 and her son, Prince Constantine, became king. Worse still, by 1967, after years of persecution, left-wingers were starting to make a comeback, something which right-wing officers in the army found particularly galling. As far as these very conservative officers were concerned, there was nothing much to choose between a mild liberal, perhaps calling for divorce on demand, and a raving communist demanding a Stalinist state. Both were guilty of undermining traditional Greek values.

The American CIA, which was very busy in Greece, had been getting reports about a military plot for some time but, as far as they could make out, the plotters were undecided as to which of them should make the first move. At a secret meeting on 20 April, a group of senior Generals agreed not to do anything until May. It was at this point that fate, or perhaps a malicious onlooker, stepped in. A certain Colonel Georgios Papadopoulos, who had not been invited to the meeting, was told that the wife of an acquaintance had received, apparently by mistake, a short, breathless, anonymous phone call:

They will strike tonight.

Papadopoulos had had enough of waiting. He put the word out to associates that *he* would 'strike tonight'. In the early hours of 21 April 1967, tanks moved into Athens and parked menacingly in the central Syntagma Square before the parliament building. Over the next five hours, using a long-prepared list of names, Colonel Yannis Ladas and his men rounded up ten thousand 'enemies of the state'. Ladas later boasted:

> *My plan was carried out with mathematical precision ... very simple, diabolical.*

The 'Colonels' Coup' to 'save the country from communism' had been successfully accomplished.

If you're in Athens
The Greek Parliament building is situated in Syntagma Square and is guarded by the traditionally-dressed National Guard (*evzones*) in their skirts and pom-pom clogs. The changing of the guard takes place on Sundays at 11.00.

The king and the coup

King Constantine had just gone to bed in his palace at Tatoi when the phone rang bringing news of the coup. He fell into a turmoil, not knowing what to do for the best. All was confusion. Even Papadopoulos, the coup leader, was making up the script as he went along though wearing his habitual dark glasses so as to look inscrutable. One thing was clear to Constantine - bloodshed had to be avoided at all costs. To keep the Colonels happy, he agreed to be photographed with them on the palace steps. As a piece of propaganda for the Colonels, the photo was second to none. The picture was flashed to news agencies around the world as 'proof' that the king was backing the coup.

Constantine was deeply unhappy about the coup and about how he had been tricked into appearing to support it. He launched a desperate counter-coup that December, but the Colonels' spies had taken to tapping his phone calls and knew all about it in advance. It was a miserable failure. The king's small band of loyal officers were rounded up. With snow swirling round their two small planes, the king and his family, with their friends, supporters and spare jewellery flew out from the small aerodrome at Kavalla to the exile that they remain in to this day.

Talking fridges

In other parts of the world, 1967 was the 'Summer of Love'. People gawped at Greece in amazement as the weird, stiffly-uniformed colonels outlawed long hair, miniskirts and bearded foreigners and generally waged war on the modern world. Brigadier-General Pattakos even banned the 'subversive' soundtrack of the family film, *Zorba the Greek.*

Much of the underground opposition to the regime had a peaceful, faintly hippy tinge. The aim was to deflate rather than destroy. In one surreal campaign, tape recorders were slipped into the fridges on sale outside appliance shops in Athens. Timers activated the tapes and the machines would blare out at random: 'This is your talking fridge! Down with Papadopoulos! Down with the junta! Long live democracy!'

But the Colonels were no laughing matter. They outlawed trades unions and communists, sacked thousands of civil servants, judges, teachers and university professors and clamped down hard on the press. The old Civil War prison islands opened for business again and brutality, torture, disappearances and murder were the everyday tools of their trade. Unsurprisingly, the regime had no real popular support. It was only through fear, bribery and massive borrowing to buy public acquiescence that the military junta was able to hang on to power for six years.

Regime change

Things started to go wrong for the colonels in 1973. Student demonstrations and sit-ins began in January and were a thorn in the Colonels' side for most of the year. In May, there was a monarchist-inspired naval mutiny and Papadopoulos abolished the monarchy and declared himself lifetime President - which did nothing for his popularity ratings. In November, tanks stormed Athens University and the student occupations were brutally crushed. Thirty students died. Frightened of a public backlash, Papadopoulos was overthrown by another Colonel, Dimitrios Ioannides.

Ioannides was even more dull-witted than Papadopoulos. It was patently obvious to everyone that the regime was an unpleasant irrelevance which had run out of steam. Even the Colonels' own henchmen began refusing to obey orders and the regime fell apart at the seams. With nobody in charge of the country, a few of the more sensible Colonels realized that the game was up. They begged a respected former Prime Minister, Konstantinos Karamanlis to come home from exile and he duly took charge on 25 July 1974.

The seven-year nightmare was over.

Peace and Quiet ...

... SORT OF!

Dumping the past ...

And on 29 August 1989, forty years to the day since the last battle of the Civil War, sixteen and a half million secret files were dredged out of the basement of the Security Police HQ in Athens. They were carried ceremoniously in a fleet of specially chartered trucks to a steel mill north of the city. There, the files on soldiers, politicians, musicians, actors, and thousands of ordinary citizens were dropped into a huge furnace, burned, and were gone forever.

President Konstantinos Karamanlis had done a brilliant job in tidying up the mess left by the Colonels. Most of them had been rounded up, put on trial and sentenced to life imprisonment soon after he came to power and, by 1989, Greece was a different and kinder country. Religious freedom had been guaranteed by statute for the first time, the Communist party had been unbanned and Greece had joined the European Union (1981).

But history is still history, and other legacies live on. As recently as 1999 there was nearly another war between old adversaries when Turkey accused Greece of harbouring Kurdish terrorists. Both countries started an arms race until, on 17 August, nature intervened. A massive earthquake struck western Turkey and, in a heartwarming display of humanity, the Greeks put their weapons aside and sent rescue workers to the disaster zone. Then on 7 September, an earthquake struck Athens - and the Turks in turn rushed aid to Greece.

This spontaneous display of 'earthquake diplomacy' has helped more than any amount of diplomatic sparring to bring the two countries closer together.

... and looking to the future

Despite a few rumbling bones of contention - especially Cyprus, partitioned for over thirty years - the future looks bright for Greece. As rank outsiders, the Greek football team were shock winners of Euro '04, and, against many people's expectations, the 2004 Olympics were a brilliant success. The infamous Athens smog is getting sorted out too.

There's still hardly any industry, but who needs industry when there's plenty of other things to offer such as: sun, sea, sand and scenery, romantic ruins, fantastic food, colourful and welcoming people, the list is almost endless.

Pass the ouzo!

Antío!
(Goodbye!)

HEADS OF STATE OF GREECE SINCE 1821

Leaders during the War of Independence
1821-22	Anarchic period
1822-28	Annual 'Presidents of the Executive'
1828-31	President Ioannis Kapodistrias (assassinated)
1831-33	Anarchic period

Greek Monarchy
1833-62	King Otto I (of Bavarian Royal House) (abdicated)
1863	Anarchic period
1863-1913	George I (of Danish Royal House) (assassinated)
1913-17	Constantine I (abdicated)
1917-20	Alexander I (died of monkey bite)
1920-22	Constantine I (restored then abdicated again)
1922-24	George II (deposed1922, monarchy abolished 1924, in exile 1922-35)

Greek Republic
1923	Revolutionary Committee of Nikolaos Plastiras and Stilianos Gonatos
1924	President Paul Konduriotis (deposed)
1924-26	Theodoros Pangalos (unelected dictator)
1926-29	President Paul Konduriotis
1929-35	President Alexander Zaimis

Restored Monarchy
1935	Georgios Kondylis (October to November as Regent)

1935-47	George II ('ruled' from abroad 1941-46)
[1936-41	Dictator Ioannis Metaxas]
1947-64	Paul I
1964-73	Constantine II (deposed and exiled 1967, monarchy abolished 1973)

'The Colonels' Period

1967-72	George Zoitakis ('Regent' for Constantine)(ousted)
1972-73	Georgios Papadopoulos (so-called 'Regent' for Constantine)
1973	President Georgios Papadopoulos (ousted)
1973-74	President Phaidon Gizikis (ousted) and Dimitrios Ioannides (ousted)

Hellenic Republic

1974	Konstantinos Karamanlis (Acting Head of State)
1974-75	President Michael Stasinopoulos
1975-80	President Konstantinos Tsatsos
1980-85	President Konstantinos Karamanlis
1985-90	President Christos Sarzetakis
1990-95	President Konstantinos Karamanlis
1995-2005	President Konstantinos Stephanopoulos
2005	-President Karolos Papoulias

SOME IMPORTANT DATES

Stone Age (BC)

350,000	Earliest humans in Thessaly.
100,000	Neanderthal hunters in Epirus.
6500	Stone-Age farming in Thessaly.

Bronze Age (BC)

3300	Bronze Age starts on mainland, the Cyclades and Crete.
2100-1650	First Minoan Palace Culture on Crete.
1650-1500	Second Minoan Palace Culture on Crete.
1500-1200	Third Minoan Palace Culture on Crete.
c1625	Thera volcano (Santorini) erupts.
1600	Mycenaeans arrive from the north and build 'Cyclopean' walls (on the mainland).
1200-1050	Decline of Myceneans.
1184	Traditional date for the fall of Troy.
1200-1000	Dorian invasions from the north, settling mainland, Crete and Asia Minor.
1050-750	Large population movements from mainland to the Islands and Asia Minor.

Archaic Age (BC)

950	Iron Age starts in Greece.
800	City states start. Greek colonies founded around Mediterranean and Black Sea.
776	Traditional date for the first Olympic Games.

c750-700	Poet Homer probably active.
c700-650	Poet Hesiod probably active.
625	Sparta and Athens begin to dominate Greece. Democracy in some city states.
c620	Greek coinage first minted.
550-497	Mathematician Pythagoras (582-497) active.
545	Persians under Cyrus the Great conquer Ionian Greeks in Asia Minor.
513	Persians under Darius I invade Thrace.
499	Ionian revolt.
494	Ionian revolt crushed by Persians under Darius I. City of Miletus destroyed.
492	Persians under Darius I invade the Greek mainland.
490	Battle of Marathon won by Athenians.
480	Battle of Thermoplylae against the Persians under Xerxes: Greeks defeated.
479	Battle of Salamis won by Greek navy. Battles of Plataea and Mycale against Persians won by Greeks.

Classical Age (BC)

479-385	Major playwrights active: Aeschylus (525-456), Sophocles (496-406), Euripedes (485-406), Aristophanes (445-385).
478	Delian League formed: an alliance of Greek states to counter Persians.
472-460	The Delian League gradually becomes an Athenian Empire, causing a series of revolts against Athenian rule.

467	Cimon of Athens destroys the Persian navy: end of Persian threat.
461-429	Democratic leader Pericles in charge of Athens.
460-446	First Peloponnesian War between Athens and Sparta.
447-432	Parthenon and other works in Athens built.
445-425	Herodotus, 'The Father of History' (485-425), active.
432-399	The philosopher Socrates (469-399) active.
431-404	Second Peloponnesian War: Sparta against Athens. Athens defeated.
404-371	Sparta dominant in Greece.
396-347	The philosopher Plato (c428-c348) active.
395-386	Corinthian War: Athens and allies against Sparta.
371-362	Thebans win Battle of Leuctra, ending Spartan domination of Greece. Thebes becomes dominant state in Greece.
359-336	Reign of King Philip II of Macedonia. Begins wars against the Greeks.
350-322	Philosopher Aristotle (384-322) active.
338	Philip II wins Battle of Khaironeia against Athens and Thebes.
337	'Hellenic League' of Greek states formed under Macedonian control.

Hellenistic Age (BC)

336-323	Reign of Alexander the Great.
323-240	Macedonian Empire divided into four

	large kingdoms. Greek becomes major language in the Middle East.
262-212	Greek mathematician and engineer Archimedes (287-212) active.
221-179	Reign of King Philip V of Macedonia.
215-205	Alliance between Philip V and Hannibal leading to First Macedonian War against the Romans.
200-197	Second Macedonian War.
179-168	Reign of King Perseus, last king of Macedonia.
146	Corinth destroyed by Romans, confirming Roman rule throughout Greece.

Roman Greece (AD)

66-67	Emperor Nero visits Greece.
306-37	Reign of Constantine the Great.
330	Constantinople founded.
392	293rd and last Ancient Olympic Games.
393	Olympic Games abolished by Emperor Theodosius I.
395	Formal split of Eastern and Western Roman Empires.
441-47	Attila the Hun rampages through the Balkans.
532	Nika Revolt: Blues and Greens destroy centre of Constantinople.
532-37	Reconstruction of Haghia Sophia in Constantinople by Justinian I.
533-49	General Belisarius reconquers much of Western Roman Empire.
638-78	Muslim Arabs conquer Jerusalem, Egypt, Asia Minor.
671-78	First Arab siege of Constantinople.
717-18	Second Arab siege of Constantinople.

1061-91	Normans active in Mediterranean, attacking Sicily and Greece.
1065	Seljuk Turks invade Asia Minor.
1201-04	Fourth Crusade and the sack of Constantinople.
1261	Byzantines retake Constantinople.
1354	Ottoman Turks capture Gallipoli.
1453	Ottoman Sultan Mehmet II captures Constantinople.
1461	Ottoman Turks take Trebizond, last Greek outpost of the Byzantine Empire.

Ottoman Rule

1520-66	Reign of Suleiman the Magnificent.
1523	Ottomans capture Rhodes from the Crusader Knights of St John.
1570	Turks under Selim the Sot capture Cyprus.
1571	Battle of Lepanto.
1814	'Friendly Society' formed in Greece.
1820	Sultan sends troops to crush Ali Pasha.
1821	Alexandros Ipsilantis starts War of Independence in the north. Bishop Germanos raises revolutionary flag in the south.
1822	Ali Pasha killed. Major fighting between Greeks and Turks in Greece.
1824	Lord Byron dies at Mesolongi.
1827	Battle of Navarino.

Modern Greece

1827-31	Ioannis Kapodistrias elected first president, ends War and is assassinated.
1832-6	Reign of King Otto of the Greeks.
1853-57	Crimean War: Greek involvement

	stopped by French and British blockade.
1863-1913	Reign of King George of the Hellenes.
1864	Ionian Islands ceded by Britain to Greece.
1868-90	Archaeologist Heinrich Schliemann digs in Greece and Asia Minor.
1881	Congress of Berlin: Ottomans cede southern Thessaly to Greece.
1893.	Opening of Corinth Canal.
1896	First Modern Olympic Games held in Athens.
1897	Major military defeat by Turks in northern Greece.
1899-1935	Archaeologist Sir Arthur Evans digs in Crete.
1909	Army coup by Military League.
1910-35	Eleftherios Venizelos active in mainland Greek politics.
1911-13	Balkan Wars. Northern Thessaly and Crete become part of Greece.
1913-17	First reign of King Constantine I.
1917-20	Reign of King Alexander.
1914-18	First World War. Eastern Thessaly captured by Greece.
1916-20	'National Schism'.
1919-22	War with Turkey. Burning of Smyrna marks end of *Megali Idea*.
1920-22	Second reign of King Constantine I.
1922-23	First reign of King George II
1923-35	Republic in Greece.
1935-47	Second reign of King George II.
1935-41	Dictatorship of Ioannis Metaxas.
1939-45	Second World War.
1943-49	Greek Civil War.

1947	Dodecanese Islands ceded to Greece by Italy. Current Greek borders fixed.
1947-64	Reign of King Paul.
1964-73	Reign of King Constantine II.
1967-74	'The Colonels' period: military junta rules Greece. Monarchy abolished in 1973.
1981	Greece joins European Union.
1999	'Earthquake Diplomacy' with Turkey.
2001	Greece joins euro zone, signalling end of the drachma.
2004	Greece wins Euro 2004 football tournament.
2004	Athens hosts the Olympic Games.

INDEX